Love is the highest emotion humans are capable of.
I'll keep looking until I find my genuine soul mate.* Until then, I'll be patient.
Mountain of Love
Love is overrated. Nobody needs love to have a successful marriage.
I love everybody!
I'm in a very happy, loving relationship. I hope it lasts.
I gave up on love. I've had my heart broken too many times.

- I'm schizophrenic*, so I just don't fit into society.
- I suffer from bipolar disorder*, so I can't adjust.
- I'm delusional*. I see the world as I wish it to be.
- I'm depressed because the world isn't like it should be.
- The doctors say I'm anorexic*, but I thought I was just hungry.
- I'm a drug addict, but I don't know why I'm here. Do they lock up cancer patients?
- I'm not crazy! It's just more convenient for the establishment* to put me here because they don't know what else to do with me.
- I gave away all my money to the poor, so they said I MUST be insane.
- I might be nuts* but I'm saner than the doctor and the judge who put me here.
- They wanted me to get well. But then why did they put me here with all these sick people?

Well, of course the government has an obligation to help the poor, but we must also protect the nation's assets and promote everyone's freedom to improve themselves by succeeding in business. Taxes are a job-killer. Only rich people can hire poor people. The government wastes too much of its income on programs that don't actually work. Too many able-bodied poor people just play the system on their own behalf and collect unnecessary welfare. People need to make good choices in life and stop blaming everyone else for their bad choices. People must be self-sufficient and should not expect a handout.

As the spokesperson for the poor in this country, I'm telling you both that the only way to lift us out of poverty is by giving us a good education and better jobs and that means investing in the future. That means higher taxes, especially on the richest ones.

The poor people demand government support, and the politicians pretend to listen to them while never actually doing anything but make excuses. I've heard it all a million times before, and I'm a bit bored by the whole conversation. But everyone knows the politicians are just doing the jobs we rich people hire them to do—protect our wealth.

I'm a slave to a schedule imposed on me by invisible bosses. Someone tells me what time I'm supposed to be at work, what time I'll leave, when I'll eat, what tasks I have to perform there, how to do them, what to wear, who to talk to. Sometimes I wish I had control over my own destiny and could do as I pleased.

I'm as free as a bird, and as broke. I absolutely do whatever I want to do, whenever I wish, as long as it doesn't cost any money. I have lots of casual friends who envy my independence, but it's hard to have any enduring* relationships when I don't have any stability in life. Freedom isn't free.

The Best Reading & Discussion Textbook for

Intermediate and Advanced English Users!!!

3rd Edition
All New

EXPRESS YOURSELF 2

15 Practical Topics 15 Dialogs

554 Questions to Make You Think
30 Opinion Samples
Plus 180 Captions
Everything You Need to Learn Real English!
Express Yourself & Improve Yourself

Written by LIS KOREA Editorial Staff &
Duane Vorhees

Introduction

NEW: Something that is fresh.

EXPRESS: Fast, direct.

YOURSELF: The most important part of the title, actually. Like the "old" EXPRESS YOURSELF, the new one inspires you to be YOURSELF. Unlike the pre-programmed, robotic texts in common use, NEW EXPRESS YOURSELF encourages you to use English to express your own ideas, emotions, and personality. It insists that you be YOURSELF, not just an anonymous cog in a wheel or a rat in a maze. Other books can provide you with English grammar, but NEW EXPRESS YOURSELF lets you actually use the language you've learned. If you are too self-consciously concerned about making minor syntactical or verbal mistakes, you will not be free to speak your mind freely. So, for real discussion of important issues in your own life and in the world around you, try NEW EXPRESS YOURSELF!

Duane Vorhees

Contents

ISSUE 16

Paradox of Our Times

1. The paradox* of our times is that we have taller buildings but shorter tempers; wider freeways, but narrower viewpoints.
2. We buy more but enjoy it less.
3. We have bigger houses and smaller families; more conveniences, but less time; we have more advanced degrees but less common sense; more knowledge but less good judgment; more medicine but less wellness.
4. We have multiplied our possessions but diminished* our values.
5. We have higher incomes but lower morals*.
6. We have been all the way to the moon and back, several times, but have trouble crossing the street to meet a new neighbor.
7. We've conquered outer space, but our inner space is still a mystery.
8. We have cleaned up the air but polluted the soul; split the atom but enlarged our prejudices.
9. We talk too much, listen too little, love too seldom, and hate too often.
10. These are times of steep* profits and shallow* relationships, more leisure and less fun, two incomes and more need.
11. It is a time when there is much in the show window and little in the stockroom*; a time when technology can bring a message to you in seconds, and you can take it to heart* or just hit "delete." The paradox is having simultaneously too much and too little.

— How can you talk to me like that? I'm a very successful man.
— You aren't as successful as you pretend to be.
— What do you mean? I have lots of money and nice things.
— Yes, but you don't know how to make your wife happy.
— I give you anything you want.
— But nothing that I need.

I don't know if they are unhappy because they are married or because they are rich, but I'm content being neither.

---

paradox : situation that seems strange because it involves two ideas or qualities that are opposite or very different
diminish : cause (sth) to become less in size, importance, etc. **morals :** proper ideas and beliefs about how to behave in a way that is considered right and good by most people **steep :** very high
shallow : not caring about or involving serious or important things **stockroom :** storage area for supplies and goods **take (sth) to heart :** listen carefully to what (sb) says, and try to do what they say

Comprehension

1. Is the writer happy or unhappy? Justify your response.
2. What does "much in the show window and little in the stockroom" imply?
3. Why is it difficult to cross the street to welcome a new neighbor?

Express Yourself

1. Why are modern people so short-tempered?
2. Why are our viewpoints getting narrower?
3. If we save so much time with devices like washing machines, toasters, smart phones, and computers, why are we always in such a hurry?
4. In what ways do we lack common sense despite having advanced degrees?
5. If knowledge isn't necessary for good judgment, then what is? Are all kinds of knowledge equally useful for this purpose?
6. Is it true that as we make more money we lower our moral values?
7. Can any society be free from prejudice?
8. Do you think a double-income family runs a higher risk of divorce than a single-income one?
9. The government permits selling tobacco products while educating people about their harmful effects. Is that hypocrisy*? What do you think?
10. Casinos and distilleries* make lots of money and spend a small amount on treatment and rehab*. Should they spend less or more?
11. It seems salaries go up every year but fail to keep up with inflation. Is your life in the red*? What can you do about it?
12. People marry because they are in love but then divorce for love of someone else. What can be done about this?
13. People have babies for joy but then suffer for them. Is having babies worth the sacrifice in terms of worry and expense?
14. Some criminals are being released before their sentences are up* simply because prisons are too crowded. What solution would you propose?
15. Prisons may have become the graduate schools for more effective criminal behavior. Do you believe prisons do a good job of rehabilitation*? Are there any other options?
16. If the rich would only be a little bit more generous toward the poor, our world would be a much more enjoyable place to live. But they don't seem to be so. Why don't rich people help the poor more?

---

hypocrisy : practice of professing beliefs, feelings, or virtues that (sb) does not hold or possess **distillery :** place where alcoholic drinks are produced **rehab :** program for helping people who have problems with drugs, alcohol, etc. **in the red :** spending and owing more money than is being earned **up :** at an end; finished **rehabilitate :** bring (sb/sth) back to a normal, healthy condition after an illness, injury, drug problem, etc.

Opinion Samples

1. Governments often have competing interests*. On the one hand, tobacco farmers, brewers, and smut peddlers* provide legal products that are in public demand. If their activities became illegal, the demand would not simply disappear, but unemployment figures would rise and tax revenues would shrink*. On the other hand, consumers have a need to get reliable information about health (and other) matters, and in the long run it is cheaper for society to try to treat and rehabilitate the people who use those products than to ignore them or litigate* against them. Governments, typically, try to sustain* the economy while also dealing with the negative effects of bad behavior, while also trying to promote public morality and decency, while also keeping the populace content*. In my opinion, governments should permit most kinds of immoral behavior, such as prostitution, polygamy, and drug use, but impose high "sin taxes" and use the proceeds* for educational, treatment and other restitutive* programs.

2. I can't afford to pay all at once* for tuition, medical care, health club membership, counseling, rent, food, and entertainment. But if I am convicted of a crime and sent to prison, I can get all of these — plus personal armed security! — for free. I would lose my good reputation and a few years of freedom, but the investment would pay off: I would have a degree, or at least college credits and certification of skills, and I would be in improved physical condition, and I would not have had to pay anything for rent and food, so I would still have whatever money I had in savings. But, even though my earning potential would have improved dramatically, I wonder if rehabilitation would be worth the effort. After all, the longer I stayed in prison, the longer I would enjoy the benefits, and I would not have to worry about being laid off or evicted*. Maybe recidivism* is the smart thing.

Dialog

Are We Happier Than We Were 100 Years Ago?

Harold : What's this world coming to?
Maud : I don't know.
Harold : A hundred years ago, people were kinder toward one another. They had genuine personal relationships, not cyber contacts between fraudulent* avatars*.
Maud : A century ago, people abused* each other on a regular basis. The social media we have now allow people to expand their circle of relationships beyond their immediate family, neighbors, and colleagues.
Harold : Families were a lot closer then.

---

competing interests : two or more interests that cannot all be right or accepted at the same time
smut peddlers : sellers of "soft" pornography   shrink : become smaller in amount, size, or value
litigate : make (sth) the subject of a lawsuit   sustain : provide what is needed for (sb/sth) to exist, continue, etc.
keeping the populace content : keeping the people satisfied   proceeds : money obtained from an event or activity   restitutive : giving back (sth) that was lost or stolen to its owner   all at once : at the same time
evict : legally force (sb) to leave the house they are living in   recidivism : act of doing illegal things again, even after they have been punished   fraudulent : intended to deceive (sb) illegally, in order to gain money, power, etc.
avatar : (sth) that represents a type of person, an idea, or a quality   abuse : treat (sb) in a harsh or harmful way

Maud : They were "closer" because they had less freedom and fewer choices. Marriages were arranged; personal feelings were irrelevant*. Divorce was almost impossible. There were lots of children, but they were regarded mostly as economic assets.

Harold : But today they are economic hindrances*!

Maud : But if so, they are voluntary hindrances. People are free to abstain* from having kids if they so desire, with very little social pressure to conform*. So, if they have children, they understand the economic burden they impose and decide to have them anyway. So they probably love and cherish them all the more despite the financial hardship.

Harold : My grandparents and great-grandparents were a lot more religious than people now, and society was more moral as a result.

Maud : I agree that religion has some impact on morality, but it's certainly not a one-to-one* relationship. I know lots of atheists* who are among the most ethical people on the planet, while religious fanatics* are killing thousands of innocents.

Harold : Will you at least agree that people had more privacy then?

Maud : Yes. They certainly did. But one side effect of that was that crooked* public officials could better hide their corruption from the public.

Harold : People didn't go to psychiatrists for "therapy" then, like they do now.

Maud : There weren't many psychiatrists available then, but that doesn't mean that people didn't need their services just as much as now.

Harold : A hundred years ago, a man could speak his mind freely without being contradicted* by a woman!

Maud : So, the last century has seen good progress for women's rights and a diminution* of patriarchy*. Is that what you mean?

QUESTIONS

1. In what ways do you think the world is a better place now than it was a century ago?
2. In what ways do you think we have lost ground* compared to 100 years ago?
3. What do you think our grandchildren will have to say about our attitudes and behavior when they look back on it a century from now?

---

irrelevant : not important **hindrance :** (sb/sth) that makes a situation difficult **abstain :** choose not to do or have (sth) **conform :** do what other people do **one-to-one :** matching each other exactly **atheist :** (sb) who believes that God does not exist **fanatic :** (sb) who has extreme ideas about politics, religion, etc. **crooked :** not honest **contradict :** not agree with (sth) **diminution :** act or process of becoming less **patriarchy :** family, group, or government controlled by a man or a group of men **lose ground :** fall behind; not do well

Read & Discuss

Can the Problems of Poverty Be Solved?

Poverty and national wealth grow at nearly the same pace. That means that while society has more money overall*, it is increasingly possessed by the ones at the top of the economic scale; it is not evenly* divided between the rich and the poor. Maybe the poor are not any poorer than they were, and perhaps are even marginally* better off, but in relative terms they are farther behind their wealthy cohort*. And the gap between the rich and poor continues to widen. But what is to be done? Confiscatory* taxes have the desired redistributive effect in the short term, but the privileged simply move their assets elsewhere, or find more effective tax shelters*, or use their economic power to get legislators elected who are more sympathetic to their financial interests. Another solution is to provide government support for health, education, housing, and other programs to create a social safety net and improve conditions for the poor. In many ways, this seems to be the best policy, but the ones in the middle and higher classes tend to grow tired of having their taxes go to the benefit of others, so extensive programs of this nature are hard to sustain. As critics of these programs point out, resources are always limited, while demand is infinite.

Well, of course the government has an obligation to help the poor, but we must also protect the nation's assets and promote everyone's freedom to improve themselves by succeeding in business. Taxes are a job-killer. Only rich people can hire poor people. The government wastes too much of its income on programs that don't actually work. Too many able-bodied poor people just play* the system on their own behalf and collect unnecessary welfare. People need to make good choices in life and stop blaming everyone else for their bad choices. People must be self-sufficient and should not expect a handout*.

As the spokesperson for the poor in this country, I'm telling you both that the only way to lift us out of poverty is by giving us a good education and better jobs and that means investing in the future. That means higher taxes, especially on the richest ones.

The poor people demand government support, and the politicians pretend to listen to them while never actually doing anything but make excuses. I've heard it all a million times before, and I'm a bit bored by the whole conversation. But everyone knows the politicians are just doing the jobs we rich people hire them to do—protect our wealth.

QUESTIONS

1. Do disadvantaged groups have any right to special favors or programs? Should they be left to fend for themselves*?
2. Does society gain (or lose) anything by trying to close the gap between the rich and poor?
3. What kinds of programs are most beneficial, or most deserving, in terms of providing relief to low-income or other needy people? (Retirement pensions, subsidized health care or housing, special education for the handicapped, job training, intervention in domestic violence or substance abuse*, etc.)

Consumers Tight* with Their Money

Reporter: Consumers are tightening their belts* as the economy continues to slump*. What will happen if they continue to resist spending?

Economist: Business activity will shrink even more.

Reporter: How can we get people to open their wallets again?

Economist: I don't know. We must seek professional advice from pickpockets*.

QUESTIONS

1. Should governments increase their own indebtedness in order to stimulate* the economy?
2. Is theft ever excusable*? To feed a hungry family, for instance?
3. Should we do more to find good jobs for the undereducated or for the ones with advanced degrees?

overall : as a whole; in general **evenly :** with equal amounts or numbers of (sth) **marginally :** to a small extent or degree; slightly **cohort :** friend or companion **confiscatory :** excessive **tax shelter :** financial arrangement made to avoid or minimize taxes **play :** use or control (sb/sth) in a clever and unfair way **handout :** money or goods that are given to (sb), for example because they are poor **fend for yourself :** do things without help **substance abuse :** overindulgence in or dependence on an addictive substance, esp. alcohol or drugs

tight : not spending money freely **tighten (sb's) belt :** begin to spend less money **slump :** undergo a prolonged period of abnormally low economic activity, typically bringing widespread unemployment **pickpocket :** thief who steals money and other things from people's pockets and purses **rube :** (sb), usually from the country, who has no experience of other places and thinks in a simple way **stimulate :** encourage (sth) to develop **excusable :** easy to forgive

Points to Ponder

1

Many people don't do anything on time, except buy.

2

Constructive criticism is when I criticize you. Destructive criticism is when you criticize me.

3

Be big enough to admit and admire the abilities of people who are better than you are.

4

Time is what we want the most, and what we use the worst.

The following sentences are all related thematically. They express a wide difference of opinions and attitudes. You may agree with some of them and disagree with others. Please discuss what you think the sentences mean and what you think about them.

5

If you wish to get along with people, pretend not to know already whatever they are telling you.

6

The busy man seems to have time for everything. The man who just thinks he's busy hasn't time for anything.

7

Philosophy is a study which enables men to be unhappy more intelligently.

8

Youth is wasted on young people.

1

down : in partial payment at the time of purchase

2

3

My counselor advises me that I need to be a bigger man about things and stop holding grudges* and belittling* people for their faults. So I decided to take his advice.

grudge : strong feeling of anger toward (sb) that lasts for a long time
belittle : describe (sb/sth) as little or unimportant

I always feel crushed by time. It doesn't matter if I have lots of free time or am very busy—I still feel squashed by time. I don't know how to get away from this "time bomb."

5

get to the bottom of : find out the reason for or cause of (sth)
beat around the bush : avoid saying (sth) by talking about other things

6

I've got so much to do. The work just keeps piling up.

I've gotta run. I've got too many irons in the fire*.

irons in the fire : activities or projects that (sb) is involved in

7

No wonder philosophers aren't very popular. They keep challenging all of my most cherished beliefs until I don't know what to think anymore.

It's nice to have the time to read a good action novel that I don't have to think about.

8

I remember the good old days when I partied every night. I didn't know time was short and that I should have made better life choices. If I had been more discreet* back then, I could still enjoy some of those pleasures now.

discreet : having or showing good judgment in conduct

ISSUE 17

Shopping

Although it is always wrong to stereotype* an individual — not every member of a group will be exactly alike in terms of attitude, ability, or behavior, and some will not share any of the supposed* attributes* — male and female attitudes toward shopping do seem predictably different even across cultural borders. Most men seem to take a utilitarian* approach: A definite product or service is sought, and it's just a matter of finding the best price or suitability; "shopping" is a chore*, a necessary evil. But most women look upon shopping as an enjoyable pastime*, something to look forward to (even if they just look at items and don't buy anything). On vacation, women go "bargain hunting" and often end up* paying more for a product than they would if they bought it locally, while men would rather spend their time golfing or reading on the beach than exploring every market and department store. Why are these behaviors so different across genders? Is there actually a "shopping gene" that determines this?

Shopping doesn't have to be hard work. I can get anything I want online, find the best price, take a break while I surf the net, watch a sports event, and chat with my friends. And I can do it all in the quiet of my own home, especially if my wife is out with her friends.

---

stereotype : decide, usually, unfairly, that some people have particular qualities or abilities because they belong to a particular race, sex, or social class supposed : claimed to be true or real
attribute : quality or feature, esp. one that is considered to be good or useful utilitarian : useful and practical rather than being used for decoration chore : dull, unpleasant, or difficult job or experience
pastime : activity that occupies (one's) spare time pleasantly end up : come to be in a particular situation or state miss out : lose an opportunity

Comprehension

1. What is wrong with a stereotype? Do you have any preconceived* beliefs about people in any particular category?
2. What is the chief difference in the ways that men and women shop?
3. What does the term "shopping gene" probably connote*?

Express Yourself

1. Do you like to shop? Why or why not?
2. How often do you go shopping? How much time per week do you spend on that activity? What do you usually go shopping for?
3. Do you usually wait until sellers offer some discount before you purchase? Why or why not?
4. When you buy something at the regular price, do you feel ripped off*?
5. Why do we sometimes buy things we do not need or even have a strong desire for?
6. "If people were able to buy something on credit*, everybody would buy everything" — explain what it means.
7. Some say they shop to relieve stress. Is that a valid* explanation? Explain your answer.
8. Should we blame overspending mainly on advertisers? Why or why not?
9. Are ads or commercials usually truthful? Do people usually think they tell the truth?
10. Which do you prefer — shopping online or offline? What are the advantages and disadvantages of each?
11. Some shopaholics attribute* their behavior to human "Buyology" and claim it is a natural response. What is your opinion?
12. Are makes* or brands important to you? Why or why not?
13. When you return something you bought, do you feel sorry or do you regard it as a consumer right? Are there any unjustifiable reasons for returning something, or is every reason acceptable?
14. When it comes to credit card debt, who is mostly responsible — the consumer, the card company, or the government? Justify your answer.
15. What's the difference between the ways men and women shop?
16. Who are wiser shoppers, men or women?
17. People have begun to rent everyday items, including cars, instead of buying them, moving us from the age of owning to borrowing. Do you think this trend will continue?

---

preconceived : formed before having actual knowledge about (sth) or before experiencing (sth)
connote : imply or suggest (an idea or feeling) in addition to the literal or primary meaning
ripped off : overcharged on credit : by deferred payment valid : sensible or reasonable
attribute (sth) to : regard (sth) as being caused by make : manufacturer or trade name of a particular product

Opinion Samples

1. I work a long, boring day under lots of stress. I see the same people and deal with the same issues day after day. Some of my colleagues relieve their stress by going out for a few drinks before they go home, and sometimes I join them, but I don't usually enjoy myself. One of my friends goes to a movie almost every night. But for me, the easiest and most enjoyable way to relieve the stress is to go shopping. I enjoy the tactile* feel of handling merchandise and the vicarious* feel of wearing different clothes as though I own them all. I like the bright lights and colors and the variety of goods before me. I enjoy the anonymous* crowd busy around me. Somehow it is all very comforting, especially if I can share the experience with a like-minded* person. Once in a while I buy something expensive, and occasionally I buy nothing at all, but usually for a very modest expenditure I can spend as much (or as little) time as I want exploring the vast range of goods available to me. It seems like every day there is something new!

2. Men regard shopping the way soldiers look at a military campaign. There is a mission, an objective, a purpose which needs to be attained. Pre-planning is important, and perseverance* a necessity. The less blood and treasure* that is expended in accomplishing the goal, the more successful it has been. Women, on the other hand, regard shopping as an exploration of serendipity*. It is the journey, not the destination, that draws* them. Experience matters more than attainment, and cost is nearly irrelevant. So, men approach shopping deliberatively*, women experientially*. Men want to find what they are looking for as quickly and efficiently as they can; women want to look for what they eventually find, in a process as drawn out* and varied as they can make it.

Dialog

James Dean's Boots

Hilda : Look at this! Some anonymous person just bought a pair of boots worn by James Dean for more money than I make in a decade!

Ryan : It's all a matter of scale. If I have a thousand times more money than you do, I hardly notice what you regard as extravagant*.

Hilda : Yes, I understand that. If you can afford a luxury car, or a dozen of them, and I have to get by* on a used compact, that's fine. But I just can't see spending a fortune on junk!

Ryan : For all I know, the James Dean boots were a good investment. Maybe lots of people are willing to pay even more for them, so the anonymous person may have made a very shrewd* purchase.

Hilda : Then those other people are even crazier than he is!

---

tactile : relating to the sense of touch **vicarious :** experienced in the imagination through the feelings or actions **anonymous :** not named or identified **like-minded :** having similar opinions and interests **perseverance :** determination to keep trying to achieve (sth) in spite of difficulties **treasure :** collection of valuable things **serendipity :** good fortune; luck **draw :** attract **deliberately :** in a way that is meant, intended, or planned **experiential :** based on experience and observation **draw (sth) out :** cause (sth) to last longer than the usual or expected amount of time **extravagant :** more than is usual, necessary, or proper **get by :** have enough money to buy the things you need, but no more **shrewd :** showing sharp powers of judgment

Ryan : You like certain brand names and are willing to pay more for those products than others, even though objectively* the quality is identical*. People ascribe* value to things; things themselves have no inherent value.

Hilda : That's a lot of fancy talk*. What are you trying to say?

Ryan : I have some photographs of my parents that are worth more to me than my expensive stereo equipment, but if I tried to sell the pictures no one would offer anything for them, and I could easily make a profit by selling the stereo.

Hilda : Even so, there is a limit to what you would be willing to spend on more photos. They might be priceless*, but that does not mean they don't have a price limit. The amount of money spent on those boots is immoral*, even if the buyer can afford it. That same amount of money could have been used for health, or education, or scientific research, or advancing ethical behavior, or any of a thousand good causes.

Ryan : You buy things that bring you pleasure, in addition to charities you support and money you invest for your own wealth enhancement. Do you want someone else to tell you how much you can spend and what you have to spend it on?

Hilda : There should be some way for society to demand some responsibility — some moderation! — on the way the very rich waste our resources!

Ryan : Actually, I think they should be encouraged to spend all of their wealth. That way, we can get some of it back from them. Why should they just hoard* their riches?

Hilda : Instead of them wasting their wealth on useless luxury, we should tax them to pay for social improvement!

Ryan : But then who is going to support the arts? Who's going to commission* the operas and paintings and sculptures and dramas that you care so much about?

QUESTIONS

1. Should you be able to spend all of your money as you see fit or should someone else make that decision on your behalf?
2. If a billionaire spends a million dollars on a political contribution, that is only 1/1,000th of his wealth. Should his contribution be limited so that the non-rich can compete fairly in the political process?
3. What difference does it make to you if I spend my money on personal pleasure, charitable work, or profitable investments, or if I keep it all?

---

objective : based on facts rather than feelings or opinions **identical :** exactly the same
ascribe : credit or assign **fancy talk :** use of academic words and philosophical language instead of plain, easy-to-understand language **priceless :** extremely valuable or important; invaluable
immoral : not conforming to the patterns of conduct usually accepted or established
hoard : collect and hide a large amount of (sth) **commission :** order or request (sth) to be made or done

Buying Out of* Necessity or Keeping Up with the Joneses*

Some people buy only the things they need, while others buy things because others are buying them even if they are not necessities. The fashion industry exists because people want to show they can keep up with the trends; the garment industry exists because people need different kinds of clothes for different purposes (beachwear, running shoes, police uniforms, wedding dresses, hiking boots, and so forth). Fads* appear suddenly, and a great deal of unconscious pressure is placed on consumers to participate. Social media users move rapidly from one provider to another for no particular reason other than "everyone else is doing it." Perfectly good brands, products, and services disappear from the market simply because they are superseded* by some other brand, product, or service which is essentially the same, "just because." A clever (or lucky) marketer manages to convince an influential bloc of consumers to buy his item and to abandon or not try a rival's item; but that does not often mean there is any inherent* difference in quality or price; and it does not mean that the marketer's new item will long survive the onslaught* of other competitors. Flux* and variety are the touchstones* of our modern age, while stability and constancy* have become things of the past.

QUESTIONS

1. How often do you buy a new game or new computer? What was wrong with the old one?
2. How many different phones, email addresses, and social media accounts have you had over the last five years?
3. What is the oldest item of clothing you still regularly wear? How old is it?

---

out of : because of **keep up with the Joneses :** try to have all the possessions your friends or neighbors have because you want people to think that you are as good as they are **fad :** (sth) such as an interest or fashion that is very popular for a short time **supersede :** take the place of (sb/sth) that is old, no longer useful, etc.
inherent : belonging to the basic nature of (sb/sth) **onslaught :** violent attack **flux :** continuous change
touchstone : standard or criterion by which (sth) is judged
constancy : quality of staying the same; lack of change

Let's Talk Funny

Heard About Shopaholics*? Now Meet the Returnaholics

Psychologist: Returnaholics are a newly emerging* social phenomenon. These are individuals who buy things and compulsively return them without good cause*.

Reporter: I don't think you need to conduct any separate research study to understand them. The explanation is very simple.

Psychologist: Oh?

Reporter: All shopaholics must inevitably* become returnaholics.

Psychologist: Really?

Reporter: Of course. By definition*, shopaholics can't stop themselves from buying things, but they can't keep hoarding* indefinitely. So in order to keep buying, they have to start taking things back, don't they?

Help! I need a doctor who can cure my hoarding. I've bought so much stuff that I don't have any room for it all. And this is all from just this week!

QUESTIONS

1. Would people join Shopaholics Anonymous* merely in order to spend money on dues*?
2. Do you regift* presents to other people? Have you ever accidentally regifted something to the same person who gave it to you?
3. Consumer spending is one of the main engines* of economic growth. So, should shopaholics be subsidized* by the government?

---

shopaholic : (sb) who likes to shop very much **emerge :** become known or apparent **cause :** reason for doing (sth) **inevitable :** sure to happen and impossible to avoid **by definition :** by its very nature; intrinsically **hoard :** collect and hide a large amount of (sth) **Shopaholics Anonymous :** organization for compulsive shoppers to resist their addiction **dues :** regular payment that you make to be a member of an organization **regift :** give (an unwanted gift) to (sb) else **engine :** (sth) that produces a particular and usually desirable result **subsidize :** help (sb) pay for the cost of (sth)

Points to Ponder

1

Bad shopping habits die hard.

2

Shopping is a woman thing. It's a contact sport like football. Women enjoy the scrimmage*, the noisy crowds, the danger of being trampled* to death, and the ecstasy* of the purchase.

3

Shopping: The fine art of acquiring things you don't need with money you don't have.

4

The only reason a great many families don't own an elephant is that they have never been offered one for nothing down and easy monthly payments.

---

scrimmage : confused struggle or fight
trample : cause damage or pain by walking or stepping heavily on (sb/sth)
ecstasy : extreme delight

The following sentences are all related thematically. They express a wide difference of opinions and attitudes. You may agree with some of them and disagree with others. Please discuss what you think the sentences mean and what you think about them.

5

Anyone who lives within his means* suffers from a serious lack of imagination.

6

If men were to like shopping, they'd have to call it research.

7

"I have enough clothes and shoes, so I don't need to go shopping ever again," said no woman ever.

8

Only two phrases can change a woman's mood, "I love you" and "a 50% discount." But not in the same context*.

---

live within his means : spend money only on what he could afford
not in the same context : not belong together or not be connected

1

Some people are convinced that the only way to cure the hoarding disease is to blow up everything and start over.

But even that scenario is probably optimistic.

2

in shape : physically strong and healthy
exhilaration : feeling of great happiness and excitement

3

I'm surprised you agreed to go shopping with me today.

It's the only way I get to visit my money before it's gone.

Hmm. Here's a good deal on elephants. Easy terms*, good warranty. Funny tagline*, too: "They pack their own trunks!" Maybe I should get one or two. They might prove handy* someday.

terms : conditions of an agreement, contract, legal document, etc.
tagline : sentence or phrase in an advertisement or advertising song that is the most important or easiest to remember **handy :** very useful or helpful

5

Why should we settle for* the worst things in life just because we don't have any money?

Nothing is beyond my desire. I want it all! And now!

We demand equality. We should be able to have anything we want. Cost is irrelevant* and it is a social construct* invented by the ruling* class to keep us in our place*.

settle for (sth) : be happy or satisfied with (sth) **irrelevant :** not important or useful **social construct :** idea that has been created and accepted by the people in a society **ruling :** having control and power **keep (sb) in his/her place :** prevent (sb) from achieving a higher social status **the sky's the limit :** there are no limits and that anything is possible

6

I'm almost done with research today, Dear. Just another hour or two, and we can call it a day*.

I'm so pleased that you gave up your insatiable* shopping habit. Now we can spend more time together doing something useful.

call it a day : decide to stop working **insatiable :** always wanting more; not be able to be satisfied

7

I don't understand how you can have a closet full of clothes and still insist you don't have enough.

It's all part of a master plan. I can't wear an evening dress to the gym, for example, so I need different outfits for different occasions. And if I have a pink dress, I need shoes and accessories to match, but if I wear my green skirt I can't wear the pink accessories. But by the time everything is color-coordinated, suddenly the styles all change, and I have to start all over again. But I know that every fashion comes back again someday, so I have to keep everything for later on, so I won't have to buy anything then, and you'll save lots of money but you just have to be patient. So, do you understand now?

8

Dearest one, I love you very much. I found these flowers and just had to get you one. It's not fresh, but it's almost as beautiful as it was. Will you marry me?

I appreciate the sentiment, but I'm afraid you won't get me a diamond ring unless it's on sale—and the only way that will happen is if it's pre-owned.

ISSUE 18

Love

No word is more romantic than love. To many people, love means everything. A person becomes happy when in love, and lonely and depressed if unloved. Love is usually regarded as a great thing, immune* from criticism. But problems arise if it is identified with selfishness and jealousy. Too many people seek to "own" their lovers, like property, simply because they are centered on their own feelings of love; but this attitude can easily jeopardize* the relationship. Ultimately*, love is based on mutual understanding and affection, and we must accept our partners as they are, not as something to be possessed or changed.

Love between parents and children is usually regarded as endless and unconditional. Nevertheless, a distinction* is sometimes made between maternal and paternal love. The attitude is sometimes expressed that a father may have limits to his love, but that a mother never can. Perhaps this is because the child was once, before birth, part of the mother's daily existence, but to the father has always been another, separate, being.

---

immune : not influenced or affected by (sth)
jeopardize : put (sth) in danger
ultimately : at last; in the end; eventually
distinction : noticeable difference between things
soul mate : close friend

Comprehension

1. What is the most romantic word?
2. What are two negative emotions love sometimes provokes*?
3. Why may there be a difference between maternal and paternal love?

Express Yourself

1. Do you remember your first love? Was it puppy love* or a real love?
2. How often do you hug your sweetheart?
3. How often do you hug your children?
4. Is there any difference between a daddy's love and a mama's love?
5. Do you think unconditional love exists? Why or why not?
6. Have you ever had a situation involving unrequited love*? What happened?
7. Some people tell their former lovers, "I'm leaving because I love you." Discuss this paradox.
8. Should age matter in love? Why or why not?
9. When a young lady marries an old, rich man, is it always because she is a gold digger*? Why or why not?
10. What do lovers argue about most often?
11. Do you think it is wrong to love someone out of wedlock*? Why or why not?
12. Do you think nonsexual, platonic* love can really exist between a man and a woman?
13. Do you think you have to marry if you are in love? What if you're already married to someone else?
14. Do you think you have to be in love in order to marry?
15. Would you ever give up your romantic partner in order to devote yourself to God or to a higher moral cause?

---

provoke : cause the occurrence of (a feeling or action)
puppy love : young boy's or girl's love for (sb), which people do not regard as serious
unrequited love : romantic love that you feel for (sb), but that they do not feel for you
gold digger : woman who associates with or marries a man chiefly for material gain
out of wedlock : not legally married to each other
platonic : relating to a close relationship in which there is no romance or sex

Opinion Samples

1. I have been with my soul mate for over a dozen years. During that time, he has patiently endured my bouts* of depression and bad temper. He has put up with* my alcoholism and drug use, with rarely a word of complaint or criticism. He has nursed me through illness and quietly paid all my debts. Through it all, he has shared our life together with a perpetual smile and constant words of encouragement. Our entire relationship has been one of unending kindness and generosity on his part. I just can't take it anymore! So I feel I have to leave him. He deserves so much more than I can possibly give.

2. Some of my best friends are women. Some of them are highly desirable, highly feminine beings, but not to me. We share intellectual interests and have compatible* personalities, and we enjoy each other's company. But we are not (so far as I know) sexually attracted to each other. If this seems strange to you, perhaps it's because you think I don't have strong male friendships or that I don't love women. Let me assure you on both scores*. I count just as many men among my dearest friends as women, and I have had my share — more than my fair share, I should say — of romantic conquests. But I refuse to put anyone into a preconceived box. I want to deal with everyone on the basis of that person's own characteristics, not decide ahead of time that, "Oh, she's a woman, so I must try to make love to her," or "He's an intellectual, so he must not be interested in sports." Humans are much richer* in their personal diversity than some people realize.

Dialog

Are First Loves Ever Real?

Zoe : You're not the first, you know.
Howard : First what, my dear?
Zoe : You're not my first love.
Howard : I would be surprised to find out that I was. You're a very warm, desirable person, and many others must have loved you before I came along.
Zoe : But you're probably my last love.
Howard : That's good. For my part, I'm sure I will never love anyone again more than I love you.
Zoe : Who was your first love?
Howard : When I was five or six I developed a strong affection for a girl in my class. I carried her books home from school and went several blocks out of my way to escort her home. But she was more interested in another boy, and my

---

bout : period of time during which (sb) suffers from (sth) such as an illness or disease **put up with :** accept a bad situation without complaining **compatible :** able to exist together without trouble or conflict **on both scores :** concerning the both mentioned **rich :** very interesting and full of many different things attentions soon passed to another girl. Several, in fact, over the ensuing* years.

Zoe : But that's just pretend* love. When we're young, we all have short-lived crushes*. But who was your first real love?

Howard : After high school, while I was in the army, I was crazy over a college girl I met. We were on the phone constantly — this was before texting or the Internet. I wrote her letters every day and visited her whenever I had leave*. We made definite plans to get married, as soon as I was out of the army.

Zoe : Why didn't you get married?

Howard : I couldn't find a job and wasn't interested in going back to school. I guess she figured I wasn't worth the economic sacrifice I represented*.

Zoe : That's probably what my first love thought, too. But actually, I was just bored with him after I got to know him. It wouldn't have mattered how rich he was, I just couldn't imagine spending the rest of my life — or any appreciable* part of it — in his company.

Howard : You mean you don't have any story of a tragic misunderstanding between lovers or the sudden death of Your One True Love?

Zoe : No, I'm afraid not. Just ennui*.

Howard : I think that's the way of first loves. They don't last, because we are naive and inexperienced and don't know anything about what love entails*. We want to believe in love at first sight, and we want fairy tales to be true. But eventually we find out more about our lovers' true nature and become dissatisfied for one reason or another.

Zoe : In order to last, I guess love needs to be based on both desire and cold-blooded* calculation.

QUESTIONS

1. Does love at first sight exist? Do you have any evidence of its existence?
2. Given the high number of divorces and extramarital affairs, even genuine love seems to have a short shelf life*. Do you agree that's the case? Why?
3. Can we love — really love — numerous people at the same time?

---

ensuing : coming at a later time **pretend :** not real **crush :** strong feeling of romantic love for (sb) that is usually not expressed and does not last a long time **leave :** time when (sb) has permission to be absent from work or from duty in the armed forces **represent :** portray in a particular way **appreciable :** large enough to be noticed or considered important **ennui :** lack of spirit, enthusiasm, or interest **entail :** involve (sth) as a necessary or inevitable part or consequence **cold-blooded :** based on facts; not affected by emotions **shelf life :** length of time during which (sth) lasts

Love at First Sight

I met my first wife in a coffee shop. I was scheduled to meet a student, but he was late. The shop was crowded, and two young college girls sat at an adjoining* table. I was immediately struck by one of them but couldn't think of any way to intrude* upon them. Fortunately, my student came shortly, and after he sat down I almost immediately asked him to introduce me to the one I was interested in. He did so with aplomb*, and soon the four of us were sharing a table, and then we went out to eat together. I don't know if my student ever saw the other girl again, but the object of my affection quickly became my girlfriend and eventually my wife. We were married for fourteen years. So I definitely believe in love at first sight, even though on many other occasions I was instantly smitten* upon encountering someone; but in all those instances, it was just a matter of infatuation* and the feeling soon passed. The difference is not intensity of feeling, but duration*.

QUESTIONS

1. Does love at first sight have to be a shared experience, or can it exist in one person but has to develop in the other?
2. How do you explain the phenomenon of two people not being at all attracted to each other early on, but then happily spending their lives together?
3. How do you explain the paradox of love at first sight and divorce? Does love at first sight imply eternal* love?

adjoining : next intrude : put oneself deliberately into a place or situation where one is unwelcome or uninvited with aplomb : in a confident and skillful way smitten : in love with (sb) infatuation : foolish, unreasoning, or extravagant passion or attraction duration : length of time that (sth) exists or lasts perspective : particular attitude toward (sth); point of view eternal : lasting or existing forever

Love at a Distance*

Reporter: Most online dating sites do not check their members' criminal history. This poses* serious problems for innocent members, who may become victimized.

CEO: Actually, I don't think it matters. We're too busy to conduct extensive* background checks on our members' private lives. But they can ask these questions themselves when they meet FACE TO FACE.

– You're such a handsome young man. I'm glad we got to know each other over the Internet.
– And you're a gorgeous woman! It's too bad we are so far apart. I'd like to meet you in person.
– Yes, that's too bad. But I'm afraid you'd be disappointed in me if we got together.
– Not at all. I know your soul. Appearance doesn't matter.
– Yes, you're right. You see me as I would like to be.
– And I, too, want you to think the best of me.

QUESTIONS

1. Internet dating has become a substitute* for face-to-face relationships. Is that good or bad?
2. People routinely* invent* alternative identities for themselves online. Is it necessary for us to know who they really are before we become involved?
3. If a con man* convinces us to meet him after online interaction, are we likely to see him for what he really is in a face-to-face encounter*?

---

at a distance : far away **pose :** present or constitute (a problem, danger, or difficulty) **extensive :** very full or complete **substitute :** (sth) new or different that you use instead of (sth) else that you used previously **routinely :** usually done as part of the normal process **invent :** think of an idea, story, etc. that is not true, usually in order to deceive people; make up **con man :** man who lies in order to make people give him money; con artist **encounter :** meeting

Points to Ponder

1

Life is short. There is no time to leave important words unsaid.

2

What a wonderful world this would be if we loved others as we love ourselves.

3

There are three things most women love but never understand: males, boys, and men.

4

Love at first sight may be all right, but taking a second look might be wise.

The following sentences are all related thematically. They express a wide difference of opinions and attitudes. You may agree with some of them and disagree with others. Please discuss what you think the sentences mean and what you think about them.

5

A man doesn't know the value of a woman's love until he starts paying alimony.

6

You can give without loving, but you can't love without giving.

7

There would be fewer divorces if men gave as much loving attention to their wives as they do to their cars and jobs.

8

Love is a battle, love is a war; love is a growing up.

1

shortcoming : weakness in (sb's) character

2

thermostat : device used for keeping a room or a machine at a particular temperature

3

hand : cards that are held by a player in a card game **butt in :** get involved in

4

thoroughly : with great care or completeness

I'm divorcing you. When you start paying me alimony, you'll finally come to realize my true worth.

You're too late. I just declared bankruptcy.

What about me? If he's bankrupt, how can he feed me? But if she can't collect any alimony from him, she can't feed me either.

6

I'll give you all the world.

I don't want all the world. I just want a few specific things, like diamonds.

7

pamper : treat (sb/sth) very well; give (sb/sth) a lot of attention and care
tinker : try to repair or improve (sth) by making small changes or adjustments to it

8

act your age : act in a way that is appropriate for a person of your age

ISSUE 19

Marriage

Marriage may be a simple matter of one man and one woman deciding to spend their lives together, despite any possible hardships* and difficulties. Usually, this means making a public commitment to each other in some sort of civil or religious ceremony. Once this arrangement has been achieved, it is usually difficult to end it. But, over time, the marriage may expand beyond a two-person agreement. Most of the time, their union produces children, and the couple will feel the need for a larger house; and there will be many new expenses that must be met*. Unfortunately, these financial burdens* may put tremendous* strain* on the original feelings the couple had toward each other at the time of their marriage. Although some couples will be ecstatic* about their growing family ties, some will find them a bittersweet* experience in which love and stress coexist, and others may find the strain to be too much to bear* and will try to resume* their former single lives. Perhaps they will try marriage again, with someone else. So, marriage is probably never a simple matter, after all.

---

hardship : pain and suffering **met :** provided **burden :** source of great worry or stress **tremendous :** very large or great **strain :** great or excessive pressure, demand, or stress on (sb's) body, mind, or resources **ecstatic :** very happy or excited **bittersweet :** producing or expressing a mixture of pain and pleasure **bear :** accept or endure (sth) **resume :** begin or take up again after interruption **cozy :** small, comfortable, and warm **mind :** object to or dislike (sth)

Comprehension

1. Is marriage a simple matter? Explain your answer.
2. How easy is it to end a marriage? Can you give any examples?
3. Is family expansion beyond just two people a good thing or a bad thing?

Express Yourself

1. Have you always wanted to marry? Why or why not?
2. Do you think you can love your spouse perpetually*?
3. When do married people most feel the lack of personal freedom?
4. Why do people prefer to stay married even though they have many complaints about their marriage?
5. Which do you think is more important, the happiness of your children or your own?
6. If you were divorced, would you remarry? What if your spouse died?
7. What spousal behavior could you never forgive?
8. What do you think about living together before getting married?
9. What do you think about choosing not to have children?
10. What do you think about adoption?
11. Why do you think the number of childless couples is on the rise? Is this related to the rise in the number of divorces?
12. What does it mean to say that sadness exists regardless of whether or not you are married? Is it also true that happiness exists, regardless?
13. Do you think divorce is easy? Why or why not?
14. What do you think about second marriages? Are they likely to be more successful than the first one?
15. Do you think "the third time is the charm*" applies to marriages as well?
16. What tips* do you have for enjoying a stress-free marriage?
17. Why do married men sometimes act immaturely?
18. What is the appeal of "bad boys" to some women?
19. Some people say they stay married for the sake of their children even though they don't love their spouses. Does this idea make sense?
20. These days a new expression has been invented: "graduation from marriage." That means that a married couple stays married instead of getting a divorce, but they lead independent lives without interfering with each other. Do you like this idea?

perpetual : continuing all the time without changing
the third time is the charm : you hope to be successful the third time after you have failed to do (sth) twice
tip : piece of advice or useful information

Opinion Samples

1. I love my husband and never want to do anything to hurt or betray him. I admit that sometimes I have fantasies* about other men, but they are all enjoyable fantasies that I would never act upon*. However, I often feel tied down*. I have a schedule that is forced upon me by married life, and sometimes I would like to be free to do whatever I like. I have old friends whom I can no longer see, out of concern about what my husband might think if he knew about it. It would be nice to indulge* myself occasionally on some expensive frippery*, if I didn't have to maintain a household budget. Sometimes I feel that I gave up my own identity when I changed my name to my husband's.

2. Speaking as a man, I can address* the issue of liking "bad girls," but I'm not sure that women are attracted to "bad boys" for the same reasons. Bad girls are briefly desirable because of the promise (even if it's only in my own mind) of wild, unrestrained sex. The more these women smoke and drink, the more profanity* they use, the more provocatively* they dress, the more likely it seems that they are uninhibited* in the expression of their passion and desire. I have no wish to marry a woman like that, but I expect she would be a lot of fun on a date or even for a long-term relationship. Her allure* is that she would be unpredictable and not boring.

Dialog

Marriage, Inc.

Lenny : What I don't understand is why you married your husband.
Brittany : I don't believe in sex outside of marriage.
Lenny : But why didn't you marry someone else to have sex with? You don't seem to like Ralph very much.
Brittany : Oh, he's all right, I guess. He's always been a good, steady provider*.
Lenny : You never loved him?
Brittany : Love is so overrated. When I was young I fell in and out of love on a regular basis, but it never got me anywhere.
Lenny : So you married for money.

---

fantasy : exciting and unusual experience or situation you imagine act upon : take action according to
tied down : stopped from being free to do the things they want to do indulge : allow (yourself) to have or do (sth) as a special pleasure frippery : pretentious, showy finery address : give attention to (sth); deal with
profanity : offensive word provocative : causing sexual feelings or excitement; sexy
uninhibited : able to express thoughts and feelings freely allure : power to attract; quality that attracts people
provider : (sb) who earns the money that is needed to support a family

Brittany : Not exactly. Ralph is not rich, as you know. But I married for security. He had a decent job and a responsible attitude.

Lenny : It sounds like you accepted a business proposal, not a marriage proposal.

Brittany : Having a successful life is like having a successful business, don't you think? You can't expend all your capital in the pursuit of some whim*.

Lenny : Well, in my case, I married for love.

Brittany : How did that work out?

Lenny : Well, you know. I guess monogamy* is a kind of monotony*. But we're happy enough.

Brittany : I'm not sure I would say I'm happy in my marriage, but I'm content.

Lenny : But for quite a while my wife and I were ecstatic* in our marriage. That passion may have faded, but at least we had it once. But you never had that feeling at all.

Brittany : Okay. If I ever get married again, it will be for love. But by then I will have saved away enough from my first marriage that I won't have to worry anymore about financial stability.

QUESTIONS

1. If you got married twice, once for love and once for money, in which order would it be?
2. Can love sustain* a marriage that has no adequate* economic basis?
3. Can a long marriage survive happily without love? Without money? Without kids?

---

whim : sudden wish, desire, decision, etc.
monogamy : custom of being married to only one person at a time
monotony : lack of variety that makes you feel bored
ecstatic : feeling extremely happy and excited
sustain : make (sth) continue over a period of time
adequate : sufficient to satisfy a requirement or meet a need

Read & Discuss

The Problems with Divorce

It is a good thing for women to have the same freedom as men, but the social effects have been staggering*. Divorce rates have skyrocketed* wherever women have gained social independence. Divorce is the legal unraveling* of a family. It has severe economic and psychological consequences and leads to identity confusion among the children of divorce and even among the estranged* couples. The problems are compounded* when the divorcees remarry and blended families* become common: Children should not be classified as "Yours, "Mine," and "Ours," they should all be cherished as beloved family members. People who expect the possibility of divorce treat their marriages very differently than those who think divorce is all but* impossible. Some bad marriages are inevitable, and divorce should always be an available option, but if the remedy* is too widely applied, it leads to social disruption* and personal chaos.

QUESTIONS

1. When we get a marriage license, why doesn't it have a renewable expiration date* like a driver's license?
2. Under what conditions is divorce a reasonable action?
3. Some religions strictly ban* divorce. Is that, after all, the most sensible attitude to take?

---

staggering : very large, shocking, or surprising **skyrocket :** increase quickly to a very high level or amount **unravel :** take apart; undo; destroy (a plan, agreement, or arrangement) **estranged :** no longer close or affectionate to (sb) **compound :** make (sth) worse **blended family :** family in which both parents have children from earlier relationships living with them **all but :** almost completely **remedy :** way of solving or correcting a problem **disruption :** confusion or disorder **split up :** end marriage or relationship **expiration date :** date when (sth) such as a credit card or driver's license can no longer legally or officially be used **ban :** officially or legally prohibit

The Big Business of Weddings

Man: Weddings have become a huge* business. Couples pay enormous* sums on wedding parties, photographs, clothing, jewelry, and honeymoon travel, even in these tough financial times. So I'm worried.

Friend: Why? Are you getting married soon?

Man: Yeah, we decided to tie the knot* next year.

Friend: Congratulations.

Man: Thanks. But statistics predict seven-digit wedding costs next year. I can only afford six digits.

Friend: So?

Man: I'm afraid we'll have to delay until people get back to the normal, six-digit-figure budget.

QUESTIONS

1. Why do people spend so much on weddings when they can be accomplished* for almost nothing?
2. Does an expensive wedding help guarantee a successful marriage?
3. Should second or third marriages be as elaborate* as first ones?

---

huge : very great in size, amount, or degree **enormous :** very large in size, quantity, or extent **tie the knot :** get married **be off :** leave; start going **get hitched :** get married **accomplish :** succeed in doing (sth) **elaborate :** made or done with great care or with many details; having many parts that are carefully arranged or planned

Points to Ponder

1

The perfect marriage would be between a blind wife and a deaf husband.

2

Success in marriage does not come merely by finding the right mate, but by being the right one.

3

Marriage is an attempt for two people to solve problems together which they didn't even have when they were on their own.

4

Why are husbands and wives more courteous* to strangers than to each other?

---

courteous : very polite in a way that shows respect

The following sentences are all related thematically. They express a wide difference of opinions and attitudes. You may agree with some of them and disagree with others. Please discuss what you think the sentences mean and what you think about them.

5

Some men believe in dreams until they marry one.

6

If all gambling were illegal, we would all have to stop driving cars. And we would never get married.

Many divorces are caused by the union of two people in love with themselves.

Nowadays women are choosier* about their divorce lawyers than about their husbands.

---

choosy : very careful in choosing

1

overlook : pay no attention to (sth); ignore

2

outfit : set of clothes that are worn together

3

bail : leave a difficult situation

5

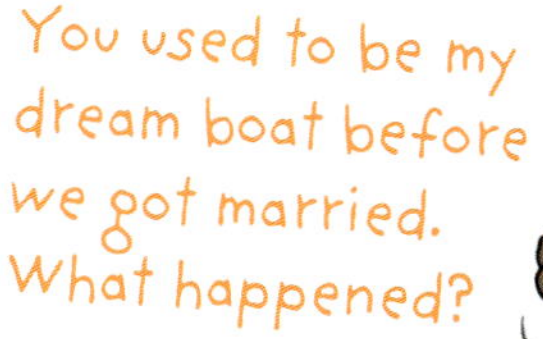
You used to be my
dream boat before
we got married.
What happened?
I'd rather be the
captain of the ship.
That way I can keep
my good looks longer.

6

Stop!
You're under
arrest!
Officers, you've got the
wrong couple. We're not
getting married, I swear!
Nobody would take THAT
gamble! We're just going to
a costume party, that's all.

7

I love selfies! And I love whoever invented them.
I'm tired of taking all these pictures. I always look the same.
Smile. Say "cheese."
I'll be happy when I can stop smiling all the time and just be myself.

Don't worry, I will.
Be careful. Make the right choice.
You're doing the wise thing, arranging your divorce details before you get married. It will save you a lot of heartache and distress later on.

ISSUE 20

Stress

Aside from the wonders of technology and medicine, our age* is also characterized* by its noise, crowdedness, and stress. In fact, the noise and crowdedness contribute to* higher levels of stress. It was possible, once, to "get away from it all" fairly easily. Most people could find a secluded* spot nearby, out in the country, in a forest, on a mountain, or by the sea. But today that is hardly the case for most urbanites*. Cities tend to have parks, but they have become very busy places with little privacy or quiet. A few cities are located in the midst of wonderful natural scenery, such as mountains or beaches, but travel to those areas may pose* its own stress hazards (traffic, crowded mass transport, etc.). In a time of unstable families, it is even difficult to find solace* in a close, confidential* relationship. And stress continues to take its silent, invisible toll* on our lives. We get frequent headaches. We don't sleep well. We feel fatigued most of the time. It becomes increasingly difficult to keep our temper or hold our tongue*. We don't smile as often as we should. To relieve the stress, we engage in self-destructive behavior — we smoke too much, we drink too much, we abuse drugs, we engage in promiscuous* activity — which just makes the situation worse in the long run. We need more relaxation but can't find it anywhere; even the old ability to "leave it in the office" after work has eroded* with the ubiquity* of smart phones and the Internet, so we now take the office home with us, and all its accompanying stress. Stress is strangling* us to death, but trying to figure out* how to deal with it just causes us more stress!

I left the Earth because of all the stress. But I didn't know it would be so dark and empty out in space. I can't deal with the added stress! But I can't go back — the fuel tank is almost empty.

---

age : period of history characterize : be a typical feature or quality of (sb/sth) contribute to : help to cause or bring about secluded : hidden from view urbanite : (sb) who lives in a town or city pose : create solace : source of comfort confidential : secret or private take its toll : have a serious bad effect on (sb/sth) hold your tongue : keep silent; not saying anything about (sth) promiscuous : having many sexual partners erode : be gradually destroyed ubiquity : state of being seen everywhere strangle : kill (sb) by squeezing the throat figure out (sth) : understand or find (sth) such as a reason or a solution by thinking

Comprehension

1. What are some of the symptoms* of stress?
2. What does "difficult to keep our temper or hold our tongue" mean?
3. What does "leave it in the office" mean?

Express Yourself

1. What is the most important cause of stress in modern society?
2. Who handles stress better, in general, men or women? Give examples.
3. Can we be stress-free? How?
4. How do you deal with stressful situations? How do you relieve your stress?
5. Do you think living in a modern, complex society is more (or less) stress-creating than in a simpler society, or is there really no difference except now we have the word and concept for the phenomenon?
6. Some say, "Use the stress to your own advantage." What does it mean? Is it good advice?
7. Some say shopping is the best medicine for depression*. Do you agree? Why or why not?
8. Is chitchat* a good way of dealing with stress? Could it be a contributory* factor in promoting* stress?
9. Some say they drink and smoke in order to relieve their stress. Does that make sense, or is it just a lame* excuse?
10. What happens when people can't handle stress properly?
11. List the most stressful jobs and the least stressful ones.

More Talking Points

Talk about the kinds of stress these people are likely to suffer:

1. employees
2. employers
3. the elderly
4. stock investors
5. the jobless
6. the handicapped
7. high school students
8. college students
9. taxi/bus drivers
10. husbands
11. wives
12. young kids
13. unmarried people
14. celebrities
15. the rich

---

symptom : physical condition which shows that you have a particular illness **depression :** medical condition that makes you feel extremely unhappy, so that you cannot live a normal life **chitchat :** friendly conversation about things that are not very important; casual talk; gossip **contributory :** helping to cause (sth) **promote :** help (sth) happen, develop, or increase **lame :** not sounding very believable; unconvincingly feeble

Opinion Samples

1. Imagine living in a society in which you knew almost everyone intimately, many of them being your own relatives, and of course they all knew you as well — your past, your weaknesses, your follies*, your day-to-day activities. You married someone your parents chose, perhaps a complete stranger. A bad marriage was a life sentence, a misunderstanding might be the basis of a multi-generational vendetta*. Imagine a time when life expectancy was what we would now consider to be early middle age. A minor wound or mild infection could be fatal. There were frequent and severe shortages of food. Education, even literacy*, was reserved* for the elite. It took days to travel even a short distance. The society's rulers were arbitrary*, willful*, often oppressive, and omnipotent*. You don't think life was stressful under those conditions?

2. When I finish my job, I feel like I have not done a day's work but a week's worth. My head is pounding*, my nerves are on edge*. So I need friendly companionship and some way to take my mind off my difficulties. So, to get away from it all, my friends and I go to a dark room with loud music. We talk and spend our money as though we have it in abundance*. Without realizing it, we smoke too much, one cigarette after another. Perhaps we share our drinks with the friendly staff, who smile at us and make us feel young again. When we grow restless* and bored with our environment, we all move to a different establishment, though it is very similar to the one we just left. When we finally make our way home, we are tired, full of nicotine and alcohol, and convinced that we feel better than we would have if we had gone directly home and dealt with the myriad* of problems under our own roof. After a short night's sleep, we reluctantly* resume the cycle the next day.

Is Stress Part of God's Plan?

Harry : I don't understand the concept of stress.

Hermione : Are you stupid? Stress is the result of social pressure. The less comfortable we are with our situation, the more stressed out we feel.

Harry : I misspoke*. I actually do understand the concept, in the abstract*. But I don't think it's either real or necessary. It's an excuse people use to justify their bad moods and bad behavior.

Hermione : There are three things I want in life: money, a nice home, eventually a comfortable retirement. The only way to achieve these things is to work hard.

---

folly : lack of good sense or judgments; foolishness **vendetta :** very long and violent fight between two families or groups **literacy :** ability to read and write **reserved :** kept for use only by a particular person or group **arbitrary :** done without concern for what is fair or right **willful :** refusing to change your ideas or opinions or to stop doing (sth) **omnipotent :** having complete or unlimited power **pound :** feel a pain that starts and stops quickly and repeatedly **my nerves are on edge :** I am nervous **in abundance :** in large amount **restless :** feeling nervous or bored **myriad :** very large number of things **reluctantly :** not willingly or eagerly **misspeak :** speak inaccurately, inappropriately, or too hastily **in the abstract :** in a general way

Hard work in any competitive situation is energy-draining* and tiresome, and it leads inevitably to stress. But I have no choice in the matter. No one else is going to achieve my goals for me if I don't do it myself.

Harry : You've hit the nail on the head*! You say you have no choice. That's exactly right! It's all in God's hands! Whatever happens to you, for good or bad, is what God wants to happen. There's nothing you can do to change it.

Hermione : I remember hearing somewhere that "God helps those who help themselves." So I have done all I can to master* my own destiny — went to graduate school, studied hard to acquire the skills I needed, worked ceaselessly on my job. And, barring* an unforeseen event like a major illness or traffic accident, I am positive I will succeed. (And, just in case, I also have a good insurance policy.)

Harry : But meanwhile you are wearing yourself out*, leading an unenjoyable life of constant struggle. Free yourself of the burden. Embrace* God's plan. The ultimate destination is inevitable anyway, so you might as well relax and enjoy the ride*.

Hermione : Maybe it's God's plan for me to toil and worry. Maybe God made me the way I am, an ambitious workaholic. I don't particularly enjoy my lifestyle, but it has its rewards. I have confidence and a sense of accomplishment.

Harry : But, as you say, you don't have happiness. True happiness comes only in completely placing your life in God's hands. Let him steer the course. Let him make all the decisions. Be happy in your fate.

Hermione : Even if God arranged for me to win the lottery and I became suddenly rich, I wouldn't be happy with that. I need to know that I succeeded due to my own effort and ability, not due to some fluke of fortune*.

QUESTIONS

1. Do you think abandoning* personal responsibility eliminates stress? Discuss your reasons.
2. What is currently the most stressful aspect of your life? What can you do about it?
3. Some of the best things in my life have occurred without any planning on my part, and some of my best-laid* plans proved fruitless*. Does that mean that I should stop trying to shape my future and just let my life proceed of its own volition*?

---

drain : use too much of (sth) so that there is not enough left **hit the nail on the head** : be exactly right **master** : succeed in controlling (sth) **barring** : other than (sth); except **wear (sb) out** : make (sb) tired **embrace** : accept (sb/sth) readily or gladly **ride** : journey of life **fluke of fortune** : (sth) that happens because of luck **abandon** : give up (sth) completely **best-laid** : most carefully made **fruitless** : producing no good results; not successful **of one's own volition** : voluntarily

Read & Discuss

Good Stress vs Bad Stress

Stress is what we make of it*. If we did not have deadlines* to meet, we would likely procrastinate* forever, and nothing would get done. But if a deadline is arbitrary* and unrealistic, nothing useful is likely to result from it either except an unfinished task. If athletes, scientists, artists, executives, and entertainers did not challenge themselves to put forth* their best efforts, they would achieve little, and our world would be a poorer, less inspiring place. But history is full of monuments to folly* that were impractical, ill-conceived*, and unrealized. For some people, stress is a spur*; to others it is a brake.

QUESTIONS

1. Describe a situation in your experience when stress and pressure led to good results.
2. Describe a situation in which stress was counterproductive* and destructive to its own ends*.
3. How can we tell* when stress is positive or negative?

---

what we make of it : we choose how (sth) will affect us [Life is what we make of it. The future is what we make of it. Love is what we make of it.] **deadline :** date or time when (sth) must be finished
procrastinate : delay doing (sth) that you ought to do **arbitrary :** decided or arranged without any reason or plan **put forth :** exert; exercise **monuments to folly :** perfect examples of foolishness
ill-conceived : badly planned; not showing good judgment **spur :** (sth) that prompts or encourages (sb) to do (sth); incentive **counterproductive :** achieving the opposite result to the one that you want
ends : the hoped-for results **tell :** see or know (sth) with certainty

Yoga Soars* as Economy Falters*

Man: With the economy still in deep recession, people are looking for more ways to reduce their stress. Yoga is reputed* to have excellent stress-relieving qualities and is becoming increasingly popular in our society.

Friend: Yoga looks like a hard, even painful, activity. I'd rather go to a bar.

Man: Yes, let's go. But the stress we destroy in the bar will come around* again tomorrow and haunt* us all day, so we'll need that yoga class to recover.

– Yoga and meditation* help me take my mind off the stress of life.

– But sooner or later you have to come back to your normal life. And the problems and the stress are still there.

– So, how do you deal with the situation?

– I just stay drunk all the time.

QUESTIONS

1. Have you had any experience with yoga? If so, was it satisfying or unsatisfactory?
2. What do you think about dancing, or exercise, as a method of relieving stress?
3. People often take up* a hobby as a way of combating* stress. Discuss your hobbies or some you might enjoy.

---

soar : increase quickly to a high level falter : begin to fail or weaken reputed : said to be true
come around : revive haunt : eventually cause problems for (sb) as time passes
meditation : practice of thinking deeply or focusing (one's) mind for a period of time, in silence or with the aid of chanting, for religious or spiritual purposes or as a method of relaxation take up : begin practicing
combat : take action to reduce, destroy, or prevent (sth) undesirable

Points to Ponder

1

Having too many things is stressful, both in getting them and in the fear of losing them.

2

Shun* the "Superman" urge.* No one can be perfect in everything.

3

Instead of counting their blessings, too many people magnify* their problems.

4

Wealth is a worry if you have it and a bigger worry if you don't have it.

---

shun : avoid (sb/sth)
urge : strong need or desire to have or do (sth)
magnify : make (sth) greater

The following sentences are all related thematically. They express a wide difference of opinions and attitudes. You may agree with some of them and disagree with others. Please discuss what you think the sentences mean and what you think about them.

5

It's foolish to worry about something beyond your control—such as your life.

6

"Don't worry" is a better motto when you add the word "others" at the end.

7

It is not stress that kills us; it is the way we deal with it.

8

The greatest stress on me in my retirement is having to deal with my loss of stress.

– Excuse me for not shaking your hand. My shoulder is giving me a lot of pain.
– You work too hard at working out. Try relaxing and enjoying yourself more.
– If I don't take care of myself physically, who will do it for me?
– But you don't need to overdo it.

3

When I worked so hard to have everything, I didn't know that would include this splinter* in my thumb! Oh! Woe is me*!

splinter : small, thin, sharp piece of wood, glass, or similar material
woe is me : I'm sad or upset

4

– I'm tired of all the worries that go with having too much money. Here! Take it all.
– Thank you. But I don't want all those worries, either. And if you give everything away, you'll still have to deal with the worry of poverty.
– Then what can I do?
– Why don't you give me half of it, and then we'll both be less worried.

5

6

— Did you have a hard day at the office today?
— Don't worry. It was just normal. Did you have a tough time at home?
— Just some minor problems. Nothing I couldn't handle. Don't worry.

7

I'm tired of running away. I'm going to stop and deal with it directly.

- I never knew retirement would be so stressful. I don't have anything to do.
- Having you around all the time certainly brings me a lot of stress.
- Is that why you drink so much?
- Don't worry, Dear. I'm drinking to give you something to worry about.

ISSUE 21

Retirement

When I was a young man I hardly ever thought about retirement. I enjoyed my job most of the time and imagined that I would want to do it until I was too old and frail* to continue. My occupation became a vital part of my identity. The daily rhythms of my employment became ingrained* in my lifestyle. I made a few contingency plans* — just in case* — but was too preoccupied with working to think about a time when I would not be working anymore. But now that I am approaching retirement age I find that my attitude is rapidly changing. I still work as hard and effectively at my job as I ever did, but the application* is a lot more mechanical* than it used to be. Retirement — being able to do whatever I like, answerable* to no one except my family (which for years I have neglected due to my professional zeal*) — now looms* before me as an exciting opportunity. I only wish I had thought more about it when I was younger and that I had made better plans.

— When I agreed to be a househusband, I didn't think it through* completely. When can I retire?

— Retirement is not possible. You aren't paying into any pension plan.

— Can I get unemployment compensation if I quit?

— Of course not.

— Then what can I do?

— You can get back to work and stop complaining.

---

frail : very weak ingrained : existing for a long time and very difficult to change; firmly established
contingency plan : plan designed to take a possible future event or circumstance into account
(just) in case : as a way of being safe from (sth) that might happen or might be true
application : set of an idea, method, law, etc., in a particular situation or for a particular purpose
mechanical : happening or done without thought or without any effort to be different or interesting
answerable : required to explain actions or decisions to (sb) zeal : great energy or enthusiasm in pursuit of (sth)
loom : be likely to happen think (sth) through : think about all the different parts or effects of (sth) for a period of time, esp. in an effort to understand or make a decision about it

Comprehension

1. What does "part of my identity" mean? What aspects of your life (hobby, religion, job, etc.) do you think define you as a person?
2. How can one's professional zeal hinder* one's familial relationships?
3. Would you describe the writer's attitude toward retirement as good, bad, ambiguous*, or bittersweet*? Defend your choice!

Express Yourself

1. What plans have you made for your retirement?
2. Are you looking forward to retirement or dreading* it?
3. Do you want to live with your grown-up children when you retire, or only your spouse, or by yourself?
4. Do you expect your children to give you some money every month when you retire?
5. What do you think about laws which would force grownups to take care of their old parents?
6. What do you think about extending or reducing the retirement age? To what age?
7. Do you think your savings will be enough to provide you with a cozy* retirement? If not, what's your plan?
8. Do you believe the government's old-age pension* is adequate?
9. What would you do if the retirement fund went bust*? How would you survive?
10. What do you think about retiring to a cheap country instead of staying in your own?
11. Is inactivity during retirement a good thing, in your opinion?
12. How will your family dynamics* change when your spouse retires?
13. Aside from* financial considerations*, is a part-time job part of your retirement plan?

---

hinder : make (sth) slow or difficult **ambiguous :** not expressed or understood clearly
bittersweet : combining sadness and happiness **dread :** fear (sth) that will or might happen
cozy : giving a feeling of comfort, warmth, and relaxation **pension :** amount of money that a company or the government pays to (sb) who is old or sick and no longer works **go bust :** go broke
dynamics : way in which things or people behave, react, and affect each other
aside from : not including **consideration :** (sth) that you think about when you make a choice or decision

Opinion Samples

1. Proposals are often put forward to delay the retirement age, since people live longer. The claim is that, as the retiree pool* grows, it becomes economically more difficult to maintain it; it becomes a nonproductive population that drains* resources from other, more vital sectors. That idea has some merit, of course, and any retirement policy needs to be carefully considered in advance. However, for the most part, the advocates* of extending the retirement age are those who themselves never plan to retire. Their occupations allow them to work even into their very old age and usually at a very high income level. They not only enjoy the challenges of the job itself, they also enjoy the standard of living it brings and resent* having to pay for the idleness of others. But most people are not that fortunate. As soon as they entered adulthood (and, for many, even before that age) they had to go to work, at any job they could find. For decades they have toiled* at routine or difficult occupations which have provided them little or no personal satisfaction. They have wasted their youth and middle age on thankless* tasks, and they are physically and mentally worn out. They would like to be able to relax in their so-called "golden years." Perhaps they want to pursue a hobby, like gardening; or travel without worrying about a specified vacation period; or read all those books that they kept putting off; or doing a thousand other things that their job constraints* had always interfered with.

2. A spouse retires and family dynamics change immediately. Someone who used to be a rare stranger is now a permanent fixture* in the house. That person doesn't quite know what to do with himself or herself, and the family members don't know how to adjust. Incidents that used to be minor irritations grow to epic* proportions. That person who used to be governed* by a schedule of daily events is at loose ends*, with no plans or obligations — and no idea how to fill the suddenly available hours. Family income dramatically shrinks*, even as there is another household member who needs to be fed and entertained. Retirement, supposedly a time of elderly contentment, is instead one of the most stressful times in life — and especially for the others in the family.

Dialog

The Best Life

Jerry : I sure do envy you.
Gail : Why's that?
Jerry : You can do whatever you like with no constraints. I wish I had that freedom.
Gail : Be careful what you wish for* — you may get it.
Jerry : What do you mean?
Gail : I used to imagine that retirement would be the way you think it is. I thought it would be a lifestyle untrammeled* by stress or responsibility.

---

pool : group of people considered as a resource **drain :** cause (sth) to slowly be used up **advocate :** (sb) who argues for or supports a cause or policy **resent :** be angry or upset about (sb/sth) **toil :** work very hard for a long time **thankless :** difficult and not valued by other people **constraint :** (sth) that limits or restricts (sb/sth) **be a permanent fixture :** be always present and not likely to move or go away **epic :** very great or large **governed :** controlled, influenced, or regulated **at loose ends :** not knowing what to do; not having anything in particular to do **shrink :** become smaller in size or amount **be careful what you wish for :** you should think carefully about the changes you want in your life because they might not make you any happier **untrammeled :** not limited or restricted

Jerry : And?

Gail : Actually, after about six months I got bored with it.

Jerry : Really?

Gail : Now I miss the old routine of getting up at a certain time every morning, having my coffee and breakfast, going to work, putting in a full day's activity, socializing* with my colleagues, and then going home.

Jerry : That's what I do every day. I'm bored with that!

Gail : I miss my old friends I used to work with. I never see them anymore. Except for my family, you're the only one from my past life that I've seen in weeks.

Jerry : If you were lonely, why didn't you give me a call?

Gail : I knew how busy you are and didn't want to disturb you. You don't have all the time in the world, the way I do.

Jerry : You're right about that! Work is killing me!

Gail : I'm afraid that not working is killing me.

Jerry : Why don't you spend more time fishing? You used to tell me how much you loved to do that.

Gail : Fishing was a great distraction* from the cares* of life, but I've found that it is not a substitute* for life.

Jerry : What about that novel you said you wanted to write?.

Gail : That was a nice dream to have. I started it more than once but could never get past the first chapter. I guess there was a good reason I never became a professional writer.

Jerry : You sure do make retirement sound depressing. But I don't want to work until I'm dead. I'd like to enjoy a little part of my life, even if it's at the end.

Gail : I've got an idea. You leave your job for four months and let me take your place, and then we'll switch every four months. That way we could both retire and not retire at the same time.

Nobody told me being in charge would be so boring. I miss the old days when I kept busy and had a sense of accomplishment.

QUESTIONS

1. How do people you know cope with* retirement? Do they seem to be mostly happy or mostly unhappy?
2. Many people are hampered* in their retirement by illness. Can anything be done to alleviate* that situation?
3. If you could retire at 40, what would you do with the rest of your life?

---

socialize : spend time with other people in a friendly way **distraction :** (sth) that amuses or entertains you **care :** (sth) that causes you to feel worried or unhappy **be no substitute for (sth) :** not have the same good or desirable qualities as (sth) else **drudgery :** boring, difficult, or unpleasant work **cope with :** deal effectively with (sth) difficult **hamper :** hinder or impede the movement or progress **alleviate :** make (sth) less painful, difficult, or severe

Read & Discuss

Can You Retire?

Compared with earlier generations, most modern people do not save much money during their working lives. They spend most of their incomes on trips, personal interests, and consumer goods, and they also run up* a lot of debt. It turns out* their timing is also off*: people who retired a decade or so ago were able to take full advantage of generous pension plans that had been put in place when they were younger, but it now turns out that (due to* inflation, healthcare costs, corporate greed, and other factors) that level of retirement comfort is unsustainable* over time, so now people have to either delay their retirement or live on less. The ones who do retire often have to find part-time jobs, so they don't actually retire at all — they just work for less money than they used to make. Soon the word "retire" will disappear from the dictionary altogether, or be considered as a synonym* for an imaginary* utopia.

retire: euphemism* for being fired because one is too old to work.

Are there any benefits in retirement?

– Only that you don't have to put up with* a nagging boss anymore.

– Well, maybe not at work. But what about the nagging spouse at home?

QUESTIONS

1. How many remaining working years do you anticipate? Do you think you will be ready when that time comes?
2. What percent of your income do you save or invest for retirement? Is that adequate?
3. Do you plan to retire to city life or country life? Why?

---

run up : get (a large bill, debt, etc.) by buying many things without making payments **turn out :** happen, end, develop in a particular way **off :** not as good as usual **due to :** because of **unsustainable :** not able to last or continue for a long time **synonym :** word or phrase that means exactly or nearly the same as another word or phrase **imaginary :** not real; existing only in your mind or imagination **euphemism :** mild or indirect word or expression substituted for one considered to be too harsh or blunt when referring to (sth) unpleasant or embarrassing **put up with :** accept a bad situation or person without complaining; tolerate

Plans to Fix* the Economy

Economist: The budget deficit is growing so rapidly it will soon lead to financial calamity*.

Reporter: Overspending is addictive, and it is impossible for citizens or their government to live within their means*. How can we change that situation?

Economist: People don't want to know the facts, and politicians don't want to talk about them because the facts are unpleasant. So the real problem is not a fiscal* deficit but rather a leadership deficit.

QUESTIONS

1. Would you be willing to pay higher taxes to close the budget deficit?
2. What programs do you think the government spends too much money on? What would happen if their budgets were cut?
3. In your own life, what wasteful spending can you eliminate*?

fix : restore to proper condition
calamity : event that causes great harm and suffering; disaster
live within their means : spend money only on what they could afford
fiscal : relating to money   eliminate : get rid of (sth)

Points to Ponder

1

Life begins at retirement.

2

When you retire, you switch bosses — from the one who hired you to the one who married you.

3

A wife's definition of retirement: "Twice as much husband and half as much income."

4

When a person acquires sufficient experience to do his job, he retires.

The following sentences are all related thematically. They express a wide difference of opinions and attitudes. You may agree with some of them and disagree with others. Please discuss what you think the sentences mean and what you think about them.

5

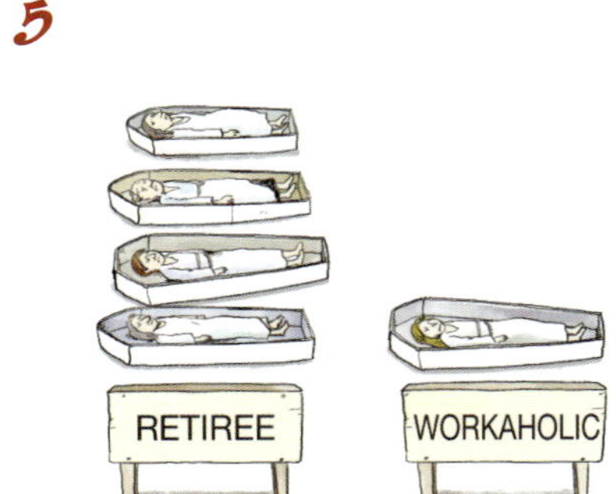

Retirement kills more people than hard work ever did.

6

Retirement: When you quit working just before your heart does.

7

I don't understand what RE-tired means. I'm already tired.

8

Sometimes it's hard to tell if retirement is a reward for a lifetime of hard work or a punishment.

1

– Hey, you bums! Why don't you find a job?
– We had jobs, but we're retired now.
– Then go back to work. You're too young to retire.
– Nobody's willing to hire the homeless.
– Why don't you employ yourselves?

2

drip : fall in drops   at it : doing some activity

3

Every time I turn around, I find my husband there, doing nothing. If I'm in the den*, he's there reading a book. If I'm in the living room, he's sleeping on the couch. If I'm outside, he's just standing around. It was easier when he was gone all day!

den : small, comfortable room in a house where (sb) can pursue an activity in private

4

mandatory : required by a law or rule
stuck : in a place or situation that is difficult or impossible to get out of

Mortician*: I don't understand it. The funeral home is having a workaholic discount to boost* sales, but business is still slow. If there weren't so many retired people dying, we'd go out of business.

mortician : (sb) whose job is to prepare dead people to be buried and to arrange and manage funerals; undertaker
boost : increase the force, power, or amount of (sth)

Ah—this is what I've worked so hard for. Now I can read all these books I put off before because I was too busy. But I hope I don't die before I get to the last chapter.

7

Welcome to your new life in retirement! There are many household chores waiting to be done.
Oh, no. At least at the office I had a regular schedule, and coffee breaks.

8

I'm so glad I retired while I'm still young enough to enjoy it. Today I'll go to the beach. Life is sweet!
I work harder now than when I had a job, but I don't earn nearly as much money. Life is not fair.

ISSUE 22

Man's Desire—Enough is Never Enough!

When I was a young man with a job that just barely* covered* my expenses I thought that, if I could make just 10% more, I would be very happy; my needs were modest and my desires few. Now I make over 10 times as much and still do not feel fulfilled*. My first girlfriend was smart, pretty, and good-humored, but she had no interest in sports so she never wanted to attend football games with me and I soon tired of* her. I thought, "There must be lots of smart, pretty, good-humored sports enthusiasts out there," and I was right, too; but none of them have ever been perfect enough to make a lasting* commitment* to (even though I married three of them). Over the decades I've moved my residence 12 times; each time I bought or rented a new home, I became dissatisfied with my living conditions and wanted a change — the one time I found the perfect home, the neighborhood around me altered* and destroyed my contentment. It has been that way with most aspects of my life: jobs, friends, hobbies, you name it*. Many times I have found what I thought I was looking for, was happy with it for a while, and eventually moved on to something "better." I guess that is man's nature.

— It was a beautiful catch today, wasn't it?
—Too good. I caught too many. My boat is sinking.
—Why don't you throw some of them back?
—That would be like a billionaire throwing away money.

---

barely : only just; in a scanty manner; sparsely **cover :** pay for (sth) **fulfilled :** feeling happy and satisfied about life **tire of (sb/sth) :** become bored with (sb/sth) **lasting :** existing or continuing for a long time **commitment :** (sb's) decision to have a permanent relationship with another person, esp. a decision to get married **alter :** change **you name it :** anything you could say or think of

Comprehension

1. What was wrong with his first girlfriend? Was she a bad person?
2. Why was he dissatisfied with his friends?
3. Would you say he is proud of his life, apologetic*, or ambiguous*? Defend your opinion.

Express Yourself

1. Do you want to be considered gorgeous*? Why or why not?
2. Do you want to be extremely rich? Why or why not?
3. Do you want to be famous? Why or why not?
4. Do you want to know everything? Why or why not?
5. Do you want a bigger house? Why or why not?
6. Do you want a more luxurious sedan? Why or why not?
7. Are you happier when you think you have more money, a bigger house, or a more expensive car than your peers*?
8. Is being rich good or bad?
9. If you had everything you wanted, what would you do then?
10. Why is it hard to give up our desires? Is desire insatiable* by nature*?
11. Is always wanting too much worse than being satisfied with too little?
12. Some say, "The less we want, the happier we become." Do you agree? Why or why not?
13. Among our desires, which is the strongest? [For example, sex, power, money, reputation, respect]
14. Desire is the reason some people succeed, and desire is the reason some people fail. What's the difference in the two cases?
15. What do you most urgently* need? List five things.

---

apologetic : showing that you are sorry that (sth) has happened
ambiguous : of doubtful, or uncertain nature; difficult to comprehend, distinguish, or classify
gorgeous : extremely beautiful or attractive
peer : (sb) who has equal standing with another or others as in rank, class, or age
insatiable : always wanting more and more of (sth)
by nature : as a result of inborn or inherent qualities; innately
urgently : in a way that requires immediate action or attention

Opinion Samples

1. "Rich" is such a relative term*. Those who have nothing may feel that a person with one thing is rich, while "the man who has everything" may still feel he wants more. Certainly the collective* concept has expanded to differentiate* between the merely rich and the super-rich. But there can be no question that, all other things being equal, rich is better. It might be true that health is more important than money, but being healthy and rich is still better than being healthy and poor — and, in addition, wealth is a means of improving one's health that is not available to the poor. Perhaps moral character can't be purchased — but being a good zillionaire* is better than being a good pauper*, and the zillionaire has more opportunity to do good things for other people. So, I don't think "Is being rich good or bad?" is even a good question, since there is obviously only one answer.

2. Ambition and greed are closely associated*. Greed is wanting to have too much, no matter what the cost; ambition may not always have a strong financial component but cannot be constrained* by one's status quo*. Certainly, altruists* exist and make their mark*, but most inventors, scientists, composers, artists, peacemakers, and arbiters* expect to be rewarded for their good deeds. Without greed and ambition, we would still be wearing animal hides*, living in caves, and being hungry most of the time. But there is a price to be paid. We may desperately want that which is unattainable, and our failure to obtain it can embitter* our lives destroying our health, our sanity*, and our human associations*. The impossible feat* is recognizing that which can be had (and working to get it) and that which cannot (and abandoning it). Usually we only discern* the difference in hindsight*, after our attempt at acquisition has failed — and, even then, we are likely to engage in excuse-making rather than admitting the limitations of our ability.

Dialog

Money Can Buy Happiness, Can't It?

Zoe : Do you think I'm a happy person?

Ivan : Sure. You're one of the happiest people I know.

Zoe : Would you say I'm overly happy?

Ivan : I don't think anyone can be too happy. Happiness isn't something that there can ever be too much of. It's not like candy.

Zoe : Then do you think I can sell some of my happiness to others? I'd like to make some money on it and I'd be even happier then.

---

term : word or phrase that has an exact meaning **collective :** shared or done by a group of people **differentiate :** see or state the differences between two or more things **zillionaire :** extremely rich person **pauper :** very poor person **associated :** connected **constrained :** prevented from developing, improving, or doing what you really want **status quo :** current situation **altruist :** (sb) who believes in or practices disinterested and selfless concern for the well-being of others **make your mark :** do (sth) that causes you to be remembered **arbiter :** (sb) who has the power to settle an argument between people **hide :** animal's skin **embitter :** cause (sb) to feel bitter or resentful **sanity :** sound mental health **association :** connection or cooperative link between people **feat :** achievement that requires great courage, skill, or strength **discern :** come to know, recognize or understand (sth) **in hindsight :** after (sth) has happened

Ivan : Happiness isn't a commodity*, you know. It's more of a character issue.

Zoe : But I read just this morning that the superrich feel they can buy happiness. I just want to get in on the market.

Ivan : I think what they mean is that they can buy the "stuff" that most people equate* with happiness — you know, like nice homes and exotic* vacations and jewelrys — trinkets* like that.

Zoe : But those things aren't the same thing as real happiness.

Ivan : No. Those are things that may bring happiness, but they themselves are not intrinsic* to being happy.

Zoe : But don't you think I have some quality or experience that makes me happy?

Ivan : Absolutely!

Zoe : Then why can't I monetize* it in some way?

Ivan : Philosophers and confidence men* have tried to figure out, or at least market, that secret for a long time. I suppose some of the quacks* have done quite well, but the thinkers* and religious leaders have not made much progress. Happiness still seems to elude* most of humankind.

Zoe : But there must be some reason I'm happy most of the time, don't you think?

Ivan : Maybe you were born to be happy.

Zoe : Then there must be something genetic that can be developed in a laboratory and then dispensed* at hospitals or pharmacies.

Ivan : Or maybe it's just the way you trained yourself to deal with your situation.

Zoe : Then there must be a training manual that can be published and distributed.

Ivan : Maybe so. But do you know why you're usually so happy?

Zoe : No. That's why I'm asking you.

Ivan : If either one of us knew the answer to that, we could very deservedly* become wealthy from that insight*. But neither of us knows, do we?

Zoe : Not yet. But I'll keep working on it.

Ivan : Don't overdo* it. I'm afraid if you worry about it too much you'll lose your happy qualities.

QUESTIONS

1. Is there a method or means of gaining happiness? What would you advise?
2. If we can't buy happiness, is it really worth having?
3. Would you describe yourself as generally happy or unhappy? How has that affected your life?

---

commodity : (sth) that is bought and sold **equate :** say or think that (two things) are equal or the same
exotic : foreign; extravagant **trinket :** small ornament or item of jewelry that is of little value
intrinsic : belonging naturally; essential **monetize :** express in the form of currency
confidence man : con man **quack :** (sb) who dishonestly claims to have special knowledge and skill in some field, esp. in medicine **thinker :** philosopher **elude :** fail to be attained by (sb) **dispense :** prepare and give
deservedly : in a way that is right or deserved **insight :** understanding of the true nature of (sth)
overdo : do too much of (sth); do (sth) in an excessive or extreme way

Read & Discuss

Desire: Is It an Asset* or a Liability* to Men's Happiness?

In my long experience with other people, I find that the ones who are most content with their lives are the ones who are the happiest. Although they would like to see a raise in salary, they know they can get by* with what they already make. Even though they are quite aware of the shortcomings* of their spouse, they don't expect a different one to be any more perfect. Their children may fall short* of their hopes and expectations, but even so they are good kids who will do all right in life. Whatever ambitions they may have once had have been shunted* aside by the hurly-burly* of living, and they no longer seem as pressing*. They have come to accept life, with all its shortcomings and imperfections, as it is and have decided that it is not so bad after all. On the other hand, the Type-A perfectionists and micromanagers* I know are too busy to enjoy life or appreciate what they have. They need a constant challenge to spur* them on to greater productivity, higher rewards, and brighter accomplishments; without the markers of their success, and the accompanying stress, they feel empty and listless*. So, if happiness is the goal, contentment is the motor; if improvement is the motivator, contentment is the brake.

– I've decided that I must cut down the Tree of Desire if I'm ever going to have a happy life.
– Are you crazy? Without desire we can have no meaning in life. We should nurture* desire, not destroy it.
– But my incessant* pursuit of desire has been destroying me.
– Then you should moderate your desires, or change their focus to something beneficial.

QUESTIONS

1. Do you place yourself in either category? Which one? Discuss your answer.
2. Which type of person do you prefer to spend time with? Why?
3. Which type would you rather be married to?

---

asset : useful or valuable thing **liability :** (sth) that causes problems **get by :** be able to live or do what is needed by using what you have even though you do not have much **shortcoming :** fault or failure to meet a certain standard **fall short :** fail to be as good or successful as expected or hoped for **shunt :** move (sb/sth) to a different and usually less important place or position **hurly-burly :** very active or confused state or situation **pressing :** requiring quick or immediate action or attention **micromanager :** (sb) who tries to control or manage all the small parts of (sth) **spur (sb) on :** encourage (sb) to do or achieve (sth) **listless :** lacking energy or spirit **nurture :** help (sth) to grow, develop, or succeed **incessant :** continuing without stopping; not stopping

People are Turning to* the Lottery in Tough Economic Times

Reporter: People are buying lottery tickets, even though they are feeling the pinch* in this bad economy.

Psychologist: Many people are heavily in debt, and they think winning the lottery is the only way to get out of it. It's a kind of magical thinking.

Reporter: But, considering the odds* against winning, isn't it better to save your money and use it to pay off the money you owe, slowly and surely?

Psychologist: Yes, but their debt occurred due to irrational spending. So, now they're sure more irrational behavior is their salvation*.

Reporter: What should they do? Consult* an economist or financial advisor?

Psychologist: No, they should hire a good mental health specialist to deal with the root of their problem. My fees are quite reasonable.

- I hope I win!
- I need to win again. I already spent everything I won last time.
- I hear that winners all regret winning. Too many long-lost friends and relatives, too many taxes. They miss the old days when they were poor but happy.
- I'd rather be unhappy and rich than unhappy and poor, like I am now.

QUESTIONS

1. Do you buy lottery tickets? How much do you usually spend? Do you spend more than you win, on average?
2. Do you have a sound* plan of savings and investment that you rigorously* adhere* to?
3. Is gambling* any different than investing in high-risk stocks?

---

turn to : start to do or use (sth) new, esp. when you are in a difficult situation or need to solve a problem **feel the pinch :** experience the problems caused by not having enough money **odds :** possibility that (sth) will happen **salvation :** (sth) that saves (sb/sth) from danger or a difficult situation **consult :** ask for the professional opinion of (sb) **drama :** exciting, emotional, or unexpected series of events or set of circumstances **soap opera :** television or radio drama series dealing typically with daily events in the lives of the same group of characters **sound :** sensible, correct, and likely to produce the right results **rigorously :** strictly **adhere to :** believe in and follow the practices of **gambling :** practice or activity of betting money

Points to Ponder

1

The person who lives for himself alone usually dies the same way.

2

When your desires are strong enough, you will gain enough superhuman powers to achieve them.

3

I have learned to seek my happiness by limiting my desires rather than in attempting to gratify* them.

4

Every man desires to live long, but no man wishes to be old. Everyone wants to go to Heaven, but no one wants to die.

---

gratify : indulge or satisfy (a desire, need, etc.)

The following sentences are all related thematically. They express a wide difference of opinions and attitudes. You may agree with some of them and disagree with others. Please discuss what you think the sentences mean and what you think about them.

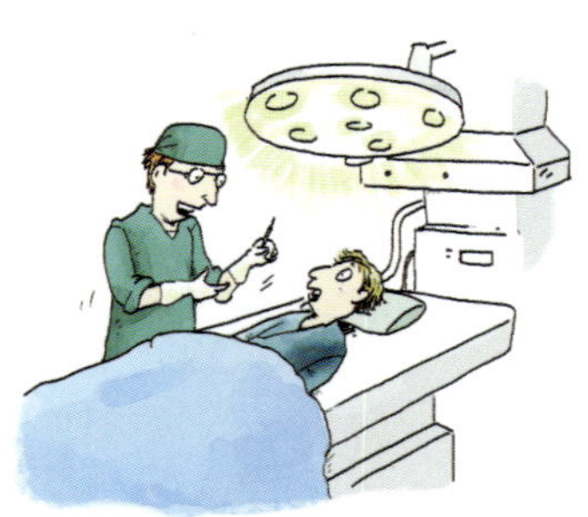

Our desire may be insatiable, but we can only stomach* three Big Macs at a time.

Man is the only animal that, once fed, becomes hungrier.

Love lasts a long time but lust only burns for two weeks.

If you're bored with life—you don't get up every morning with a burning desire to do things—you don't have enough goals.

---

stomach : be able to eat (sth) without becoming sick

1

dig (sb/sth) out : get (sb/sth) out of earth, snow, etc.

– Let's go!
– It's too high.
– We don't have any choice. But I know we will sprout* wings before we hit bottom.
– If we don't turn into* birds, we'll land like eggs.

sprout : grow suddenly   turn into : change by magic from one thing into another

3

I've wasted my life. I never found love or friendship, and I failed to get all the money in the world.

I've had a pretty good life. Lots of sunshine and joy, and enough fish to get me through* each day.

get (sb) through : help (sb) to complete successfully

– Hello. My name is Paradox.
– That's an odd name.
– I believe in the existence of mutually incompatible* conditions.
– Why, so do I!
– What's your name?
– I'm Mr. Inconsistency*.

incompatible : not able to exist together without trouble or conflict
inconsistency : quality of not doing things in the same way each time, so that what you do is not always done well and people do not know what to expect from you

5

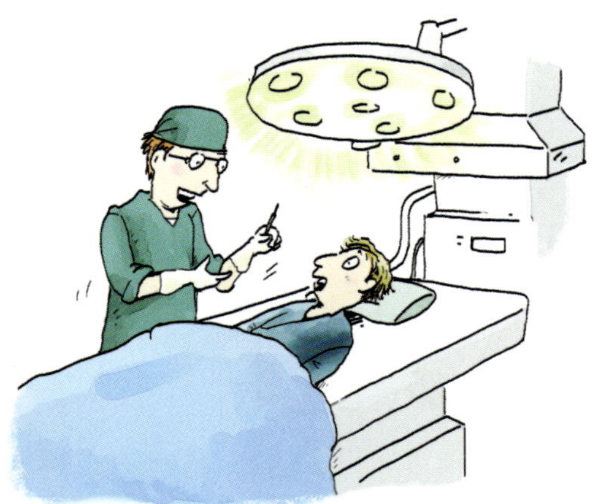

– We have new techniques to enlarge your stomach.
– Is that like liposuction*?
– No. It's like surgical luggage.

liposuction : kind of surgery that removes fat from (sb's) body

I want all the good things in life, without limits. And I know I can have them all, as long as there are enough digestive enzymes for dessert.

7

takedown : movement in wrestling in which you put your opponent on his or her back on the ground

8

– Why are you here?

– I just don't have any energy. Nothing motivates me to get up and do things, so I became sluggish* and fat. And you?

– I tried to do too many things at once, and it all collapsed onto me.

– Maybe they'll give us a blood transfusion, and I'll get some of your motivation and you'll get some of my circumspection*.

sluggish : moving slowly or lazily **circumspection :** act of thinking carefully about possible risks before doing or saying (sth); prudence; caution

ISSUE 23

Recipe for a Successful Life

Over millennia, a lot of people have gained fame and fortune giving us a lot of advice on how to live well. Some concentrate on achieving financial success, others give dietary hints, while still others concentrate on religions or hobbies. Usually, the instructions are rather complicated and unrealistic. However, the entirety* of the massive library of self-improvement cookbooks can be reduced to* a single ingredient* — love. And the directions are very simple: Love yourself first of all, and everything you do is for your own benefit. But, as quickly and thoroughly as you can manage, expand your circle* of love (to family members, friends, colleagues, neighbors, and ultimately, if you can, to all of humanity). It does not matter how large or inclusive* your circle is, the well-being of everything within it is your joyous but sacred* responsibility. Your life will be happy to the extent that you are able to apply total love to yourself and these others.

---

recipe : formula for or means to a desired end
entirety : whole or total amount of (sth)
reduce (sth) to : present a problem or subject in (a simplified form)
ingredient : quality or characteristic that makes (sth) possible
circle : sphere of influence or interest; domain
inclusive : open to everyone; not limited to certain people
sacred : highly valued and important
be stuck with (sth) : unable to get rid of (sth) you do not want to keep
primitive : very simple and basic; not modern

Comprehension

1. What kinds of instruction* have been available for thousands of years? Can you give any example, ancient or recent?
2. What is the central problem with most of it?
3. What advice does the writer offer? Is it realistic*?

Express  Yourself

1. What is your definition of "a successful life"?
2. Based on your definition, what ingredients should you combine to become a success?
3. What would your recipe be for getting rich? For becoming famous?
4. Sometimes individuals with obvious handicaps achieve more than "normal" people — why do you think this is so?
5. Are friends important in a successful life? What about family? Or does success mainly imply materialistic factors?
6. Why aren't the rich always happy?
7. Why aren't celebrities always rich?
8. Are the poor always unhappy? How can they be happy?
9. Can we call a rich man a success if he never helps the needy*?
10. How would you teach your own kids to become successful?
11. Does our mindset* determine our success or failure in life? If not, what else matters*?
12. Is education necessary for a successful life? Why or why not?
13. Is knowledge an asset* or a liability* for achieving a happy life?
14. People usually think success means making a fortune. Do you agree? Why or why not?

---

instruction : imparted knowledge; lesson
realistic : having or showing a sensible and practical idea of what can be achieved or expected
the needy : poor people
mindset : particular way of thinking; person's attitude or set of opinions about (sth)
matter : be of importance; have significance
asset : useful or valuable thing
liability : (sth) that causes problems

Opinion Samples

1. Complacency* is the enemy of success. People with great advantages may gain momentary triumphs, but without unending exertion* their gifts wither* and rot. But people with ability and grit* must constantly hone* their skills to the utmost, because they have no choice. Their options are but two: success or failure, with no comfortable middle ground. So it is that talented people with handicaps begin the race far behind the others; they stumble* repeatedly but right* themselves and continue. As they move forward, the relative importance of their disadvantages continues to diminish until it is a minor hindrance but a constant reminder of what must be done if they wish to overcome.

2. A woman I know used to be a simple but happy individual. She knew very little about the world around her and was none the worse for* her ignorance.However, she heard rumors (which were true) about her husband's infidelity* and became jealous and distrustful. She began to notice the nice clothes and homes of other people and became envious and miserly*. She learned about war and famine in distant lands and became bitter and pessimistic. The genuine knowledge she gained caused her to lose her innocence and destroyed her life.

Dialog

Does Luck Play a Role in People's Lives?

Glenda : Are you about ready? If you don't hurry we'll be late.

Homer : Almost. I have to check my horoscope.

Glenda : The time of your birth has no bearing* on the tardiness* of your arrival. Hurry up.

Homer : Don't you sometimes think that others had fortuitous* birth circumstances that have positively affected their success in life?

Glenda : I think some people were smart enough to choose rich parents, and that has made their lives easier. But not because of astrology*. Millions of people are born at the exact same time, but they don't all have the same destiny.

Homer : You have the same negative opinion about zodiacal signs?

Glenda : When you were born matters not; all that counts* is what you do with your life.

Homer : But surely you have a lucky number that you rely on?

Glenda : No, of course not!

Homer : Then you have numbers that shift* in your favor?

Glenda : I don't understand what you mean.

---

complacency : feeling of satisfaction with a situation or with what you have achieved, so that you stop trying to improve or change things **exertion :** physical or mental effort **wither :** cease to flourish **grit :** mental toughness and courage **hone :** make (sth) better or more effective **stumble :** trip or momentarily lose one's balance; almost fall **right :** put (sb) back in an upright position **none the worse for :** not adversely affected **infidelity :** act or fact of having a romantic or sexual relationship with (sb) other than your husband, wife, or partner **miserly :** hating to spend money **have no bearing :** have no effect or influence **tardy :** arriving or doing (sth) late **fortuitous :** lucky **astrology :** study of how the positions of the stars and movements of the planets have a supposed influence on events and on the lives and behavior of people **count :** have value or importance **shift :** move or change

Homer : Well, let's say you have a dream or some sort of private insight into a number that will win the lottery and you proceed on the basis of that knowledge.

Glenda : The mathematical odds* for any given number do not change. So some of the time your "lucky numbers" will win, but most of the time they won't.

Homer : I think I have lucky socks. When I wear them, as I'm doing now, I'm confident that I will succeed in my endeavor*.

Glenda : However it is derived*, confidence is an important aspect of success. However, it is your belief in the positive influence of your socks that leads to the good result, not the socks themselves. Let's go!

Homer : The world is such an indifferent, complicated place, no one can ever hope to make a go of* it without luck. So I believe that planetary alignments, the I Ching, talismans, tea leaves, throws of the dice, prayers, lucky charms, tarot cards, occult signs, comets in the sky, palm readers, and the like are absolutely necessary as aids to good fortune. I can't imagine getting anywhere without their help.

Glenda : It's a good thing that no one still relies on reading the entrails* of goats to tell the future.

Homer : So you don't believe in luck at all?

Glenda : I believe I have the bad luck of having to wait for you and your blathering*. Otherwise, I'd already have reached our destination and I wouldn't have to worry about being late!

G: I bring you wealth. If you use it well, it will help you deal with life's problems. But if you misuse it, it will bring you many sorrows. Or I bring you the sprig* of an apple tree. If you plant it carefully and nurture* it well, someday it will provide you with health and sweet taste. Choose carefully.

M1: Planting that apple tree sounds like a lot of work. I'll take the cash and take it easy.

M2: I like apples, but if I have money, I can buy as many as I want. So I'll take the cash too.

G: You have made your choice. I hope you will be happy with it, but if you are, you will be only one in a billion for whom it is the best choice.

QUESTIONS

1. Is there any difference between religion and superstition*? Does science disprove* either of them, or are they all compatible* with each other?
2. What would be the problem if reading goats' entrails was still a common means of prophecy*?
3. Can anyone actually see the future?

---

odds : possibility that (sth) will happen endeavor : serious effort or attempt derive : come from make a go of : succeed in doing (sth) entrails : internal organs of an animal blather : talk for a long time about things that are not important sprig : small twig or stem that has leaves or flowers on it nurture : help (sth) to grow superstition : excessively credulous belief in and reverence for supernatural beings disprove : show that (sth) is false or wrong compatible : able to exist together without trouble or conflict; going together well prophecy : statement that (sth) will happen in the future; prediction

Read & Discuss

Who Is Called a Success in Life?

The problem with success is that the metrics* keep changing. More and more people around the globe routinely acquire the symbols of status that used to be reliable signs of success. They have leisure, nice homes, good credit, an abundance of material goods, large incomes, good educations, dependable* health care, experience in visiting other cultures, comfortable retirements, and help with household and childcare chores. But, simply because these advantages, once beyond the grasp* of most people, have become commonplace*, they are now no longer measures of success (though the lack of them would still qualify as indicators of failure). More than ever, conspicuous* consumption has become the metric for success: spending millions of dollars on a trip into space, having campus buildings or sports arenas* named in your honor, attracting attention to the foibles* of your private life, getting your picture taken with political and media stars, acquiring new and more expensive trophy spouses*, acquiring more wealth than most of the planet's countries: These are the new proofs of success.

QUESTIONS

1. Do you think your father was a success? Would his achievements be similarly regarded as a success today?
2. In the past, was success defined differently for men and women? Has the definition become gender neutral*?
3. What are your present goals? If you achieve them, do you think you will be satisfied with them?

---

metrics : standard for measuring or evaluating (sth) **dependable :** able to be trusted **grasp :** firm hold or grip **commonplace :** very common or ordinary **conspicuous :** very easy to see or notice **arena :** building for sports and other forms of entertainment that has a large central area surrounded by seats **foible :** minor weakness or eccentricity in (sb's) character **trophy spouses :** spouse viewed as a symbol of success that is used to impress others **gender neutral :** free of explicit or implicit reference to gender or sex

Let's Talk Funny

On Aging: Does Happiness Begin at 50?

Man: Researchers say happiness begins at 50.

Woman: Aren't younger people healthier and happier than middle-aged folks?

Man: Young people aren't mature enough to know what happiness is, I guess.

Woman: Then why aren't people in their seventies and eighties the happiest?

Man: They are too senile* to remember how happy they are.

QUESTIONS

1. Do you think "happiness begins at 50"? How do lives change at around that age to make it easier to be happy?
2. Do you consider yourself happy? Do you think you will be happier or less happy in the future?
3. Are happiness and success related or separate phenomena?

---

senile : showing a loss of mental ability (such as memory) in old age in sight : likely to happen soon
liberated : showing freedom from social conventions or traditional ideas, esp. with regard to sexual roles
along the way : during a process or period of time

Points to Ponder

1

Don't make promises when you're happy, don't reply when you're angry, and don't decide when you're sad.

2

Doubt kills more dreams than failure ever will.

3

Envy is an illusion. When something good happens to someone else, it takes NOTHING away from you.

4

Success is a matter of luck. Ask any failure.

The following sentences are all related thematically. They express a wide difference of opinions and attitudes. You may agree with some of them and disagree with others. Please discuss what you think the sentences mean and what you think about them.

5

Many a man would be a *success* if only they had followed the advice they gave to others.

6

Formula for *success*: When you start a thing, finish it.

7

It is easier to climb the ladder of *success* when the ladder was built by Daddy.

8

My ambition in life was to be a failure, and in that I have *succeeded* admirably.

1

— Jump! Jump!
— But I have no parachute.
— Don't be such a pessimist.

3

It must be nice to have so many friends. I wish I did.

Can I play with your airplane?

You're so generous and handsome. Be my friend.

I wish to share my good fortune with every one!

I'll be your friend for life, if I can share your toys.

But you know that your friends care for you, not for your gifts alone.

4

Look what I found! A whole patch of four-leaf clovers! How lucky I am!

Life is not all luck. I planted those clovers myself.

dyslexic : unable to read, write, and spell

6

Here is your Golden Ladder. I built it for you so you could have an easier life than I had.

Thanks. But I want to make my own way.

The stairway to success is long and toilsome*. Every step is a challenge that must be overcome.

I'm sure there must be an elevator somewhere.

toilsome : involving hard or tedious work

ISSUE 24

Self-evaluation

I hate those formal evaluations we all have to undergo* from time to time from our supervisors or customers. They all seem to somehow miss the mark* in terms of my real performance, and they don't have the means of expressing any nuances* or any empathy* for my position. Many times, they are filled out by people who actively dislike me and can have no objective* opinion but in any case must have no more than* a superficial* knowledge about me. They cannot know my soul. On the other hand, I love self-evaluations. They provide me with the opportunity to think carefully about my responses and to provide complete and fair evaluations of my ability, character, intent*, and achievements. It is amazing* how far apart the conclusions are between the evaluations by others and by myself!

Comprehension

1. What are the problems with assessments* by others?
2. Is self-evaluation better?
3. Would you expect self-evaluations and those performed by others to differ widely or to be fairly close to each other? Why?

undergo : experience or endure (sth) miss the mark : fail or be wrong nuance : subtle or slight degree of difference, as in meaning, feeling, or tone empathy : ability to understand other people's feelings and problems objective : based on facts rather than on personal feelings no more than : only superficial : not thorough or complete intent : intention or purpose amazing : causing great surprise or wonder assessment : act of making a judgment about (sth)

1. Are you honest?
2. Are you law-abiding*?
3. Are you thrifty?
4. Are you open-minded?
5. Are you optimistic or pessimistic?
6. Are you generous?
7. Do you prefer to work alone or with others?
8. Do you want to make lots of money?
9. Are you a risk-taker?
10. Do you like to meet and talk to new people?
11. Do you frequently volunteer your time to help others?
12. Are you imaginative?
13. Do you keep promises to yourself? Is it easy or difficult to do so?
14. Do you actively invest in the stock market?
15. Do you regularly buy lottery tickets?
16. Do you give money to beggars?
17. Are you envious of the success of others?
18. In ten years, what would you like to be doing?
19. What are the most important things in life?
20. Would you be willing to give up your life for some great purpose?

More Talking Points (1)

Self-evaluation Test on Leadership Skills

1. Is doing the right thing important even if nobody is watching?
2. Do you follow through* on commitments, meet deadlines, and complete tasks on time?
3. Do you take responsibility for your own actions, accept blame for your mistakes, and have the ability to work with little or no supervision*?
4. Do you help those in need*, listen well, and respect others?
5. Are you willing to stand up* for your ideas, even if they are unpopular?
6. Do you try to solve a problem or complain about it?
7. When the situation warrants* another approach, are you able to change course easily?
8. Do you make others proud to be associated with you, transmit* to them a sense of mission, and make them enthusiastic* about their role?

More Talking Points (2)

Self-evaluation Test for Drivers

1. Does your personality change when you get behind the wheel*?
2. Should individual drivers be entrusted* to decide for themselves what a safe speed is?
3. Do you always maintain a safe distance between you and the car ahead?
4. Do you always yield* to pedestrians?
5. If the car in front of you runs a red light, do you follow as closely as you can so you can make it through* too?
6. Do you sometimes use your horn to vent* your frustration*?

---

law-abiding : complying with laws **follow through :** complete an activity that has been started **supervision :** action or process of watching and directing what (sb) does or how (sth) is done **in need :** in the state of not having enough food or money **stand up for :** defend (sb/sth) against attack or criticism **warrant :** require or deserve (sth) **transmit :** give or pass (information, values, etc.) from one person to another **enthusiastic :** showing a lot of interest and excitement about (sth) **get behind the wheel :** drive **entrust :** give (sb) the responsibility of doing (sth) **yield to :** allow another car or person to go ahead of you or in front of you **make (sth) through :** be successful in a particular activity when (sth) is difficult **vent :** express (an emotion) usually in a loud or angry manner **frustration :** feeling of anger or annoyance

7. Are you aware of the speed limit on residential streets in your community?
8. Do you use your turn signal for all turns and lane changes?
9. Do you agree that, even when passing, your speed should not exceed the posted limit?
10. Do you yield to emergency vehicles as soon as you hear their sirens?
11. Do you feel justified in speeding, running red lights, and weaving* in and out of traffic in order to make your appointments on time?
12. Do you sometimes react to other drivers by shouting or making rude gestures at them?

Opinion Samples

1. Family is important, God is important, having the respect of others is important, and performing my job well is important. But the most important thing in my life is golf. I play several times a week as part of my work responsibilities, and then I play a round or two every weekend as well. I watch all the major tournaments on TV and attend them in person whenever I have an opportunity. I subscribe* to five golf magazines and buy a lot of instructional videos. With a lot of effort, I have acquired a pretty decent handicap*. The secret behind my obsession* is simple: Golf is the only activity I know of that is not really about defeating other players (though of course that is also involved) but rather playing against oneself. There is always a new challenge to be overcome, and the obstacles are not just terrain* but also character. In order to play well, one must develop the qualities of determination, patience, foresight*, problem solving, flexibility, and humility*. These are all necessary in honoring* all those other things that are important in life as well.

2. We can defer* our commitments to others but not to ourselves. We can ignore our inconvenient promises, except when they are self-imposed*. We may be able to lie to ourselves for a time but not indefinitely*. That is not to say, however, that fulfillment is always easy. Unlike New Year's resolutions*, which are just a wish list of trivial pursuits, genuine promises to oneself are, by their very nature, both difficult and important. Obstacles are numerous and severe. So, because I am human, sometimes I fail despite my best effort, and I always feel diminished* when that happens. But one of the first promises I made to myself was that I would not ever let temporary defeat bring me down*.

---

weave : move from side to side while going forward, esp. in order to avoid the people or things that are in front of you **subscribe :** pay money to get a publication or service regularly **handicap :** number of strokes by which a golfer normally exceeds par for a course (used as a method of enabling players of unequal ability to compete with each other) **obsession :** extreme (unhealthy) interest in (sth) **terrain :** land of a particular kind **foresight :** prudence **humility :** quality of not thinking you are better than other people **honor :** regard with great respect **defer :** delay (sth) until a later time **self-imposed :** imposed on oneself, not by an external force **indefinitely :** for a period of time that might not end **New Year's resolution :** promise to do (sth) differently in the new year **diminished :** made to seem less impressive or valuable **bring (sb) down :** cause (sb) to become sad or depressed

Are You Miss Right*?

Mark : Do you mind answering some questions?
Felice : Why?
Mark : Oh, it's just a self-assessment test I came across.
Felice : OK, sure. Why not?
Mark : Just take your time and answer as honestly as you can. Are you ready?
Felice : Sure. Go ahead.
Mark : "Would you prefer to work at home or outside the home?"
Felice : Well, as you know, I've got a pretty important position in my office. But if I could afford to stay at home and take care of the house and raise a family, I would.
Mark : "Are you generous or frugal* in your financial transactions* with others?"
Felice : I try to be careful with my money, but I'm not a skinflint*. Sometimes it is necessary to spend freely on those you love, but you are not being generous to yourself or to them if you do that all the time.
Mark : "Which is more important, your own welfare or that of a spouse or child?"
Felice : If I don't take good care of myself, I can't take care of anyone else, can I?
Mark : "Which is more important, intelligence or honesty?"
Felice : We don't have any control over our IQ, but we can choose to be always truthful.
Mark : Your answers are very thoughtful so far. Are you ready for another one?
Felice : Yes. What is it?
Mark : I hoped you would give the answers I was looking for, and you have. You are clearly, for me, my Miss Right. So, the last question is: Will you marry me?
Felice : That depends. Let me give you a little quiz first to see if you qualify as Mr. Right.

— I still remember our wedding day.
— I do, too. But in all these years we've been together, you never remembered our anniversary.
— I always remembered the day but had trouble with the date. But I loved the fact that we were married.

I know that we can make it if we work together.

Oh, I hope so! But sometimes I want to be in the front seat.

QUESTIONS

1. Why don't we all administer* a formal evaluation of each other before we get married?
2. What would you like to know in advance about your future spouse?
3. Do people give pollsters* their honest views or the answers they think are most acceptable?

Miss Right : woman who is viewed as an ideal romantic partner or potential spouse
frugal : using money or supplies in a very careful way **transaction :** business deal
skinflint : (sb) who spends as little money as possible; miser **administer :** bring into use
pollster : (sb) who prepares and asks questions to find out what people think about a particular subject

Read & Discuss

What Others Think of You and What You Think of Yourself

I have always harbored* a deep ambition to be well-thought-of by others. Respect and popularity have always been important to me, and they have played a prominent* role in my rise* in this world. But sometimes I have had to make a choice, either be true to my own values and beliefs or to set them aside* to preserve others' good opinion of me. That used to present* a moral dilemma for me. After all, I have to live with myself even if I am abandoned* by all others. But eventually I came to realize that my own feelings on certain subjects are irrelevant* after all, especially if they get in the way* of living a comfortable, respectable* life. Maybe some day I will be in a position to let my real attitudes be known, but for now it is more important to be accepted as part of the community I have chosen.

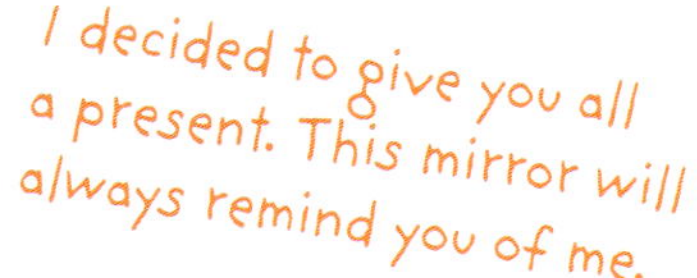

QUESTIONS

1. Are there any circumstances under which hypocrisy* is better than integrity*?
2. Have you ever told a white lie* to someone? Why?
3. If your promotion depended on a test score, would you feel justified in cheating* to obtain it?

---

harbor : have (sth) such as a thought or feeling in your mind **prominent :** important and well-known
rise : act of advancing to a higher level or position **set aside :** stop thinking about or talking about
present : create (a problem, challenge, etc.) for (sb/sth) **abandoned :** deserted; forsaken
irrelevant : not useful in or not relating to a particular situation, and therefore not important
get in the way : make it more difficult for (sb) to do (sth) **respectable :** considered to be good, correct, or acceptable; decent or correct in character, behavior, or appearance **hypocrisy :** practice of professing beliefs, feelings, or virtues that one does not hold or possess **integrity :** quality of being honest and having strong moral principles; moral uprightness **white lie :** harmless or trivial lie, esp. one told to avoid hurting (sb's) feelings **cheat :** act dishonestly or unfairly in order to gain an advantage, esp. in a game or examination

Let's Talk Funny

Not Guilty by Reason of Insanity

Judge: You're accused of forgery*. How do you plead?

Accused: Not guilty, Your Honor.

Judge: On what grounds*?

Accused: I'm insane. I suffer from compulsive spending disorder, but I have no money. So I had no choice but to counterfeit* some.

- I'm schizophrenic*, so I just don't fit into society.
- I suffer from bipolar disorder*, so I can't adjust.
- I'm delusional*. I see the world as I wish it to be.
- I'm depressed because the world isn't like it should be.
- The doctors say I'm anorexic*, but I thought I was just hungry.
- I'm a drug addict, but I don't know why I'm here. Do they lock up cancer patients?
- I'm not crazy! It's just more convenient for the establishment* to put me here because they don't know what else to do with me.
- I gave away all my money to the poor, so they said I MUST be insane.
- I might be nuts* but I'm saner than the doctor and the judge who put me here.
- They wanted me to get well. But then why did they put me here with all these sick people?

QUESTIONS

1. Is insanity a sufficient reason to be excused from committing a crime? How about temporary insanity?
2. Have you ever acted under compulsion* in a way that you would never ordinarily act?
3. If people are drunk or under medication, should they be excused* for their actions?

---

forgery : crime of falsely making or copying a document in order to deceive people **grounds :** reason for doing or thinking (sth) **counterfeit :** (sth) that is made to look like an exact copy of (sth) else in order to trick people **schizophrenia :** serious mental illness in which (sb's) thoughts and feelings are not based on what is really happening around them **bipolar disorder :** mental disorder marked by alternating periods of elation and depression **delusional :** having false ideas or beliefs caused by mental illness **anorexia :** mental illness that makes (sb) stop eating because they believe they are fat and want to be thin **the establishment :** group in a society exercising power and influence over matters of policy or tastes, and seen as resisting change **nuts :** crazy **compulsion :** strong and unreasonable desire to do (sth) **excused :** justified

Points to Ponder

1

The problem with the world is that the intelligent people are full of doubts while the stupid ones are full of confidence.

2

When nothing goes right, go left.

3

Draw from others the lesson that may profit yourself.

4

Be strong enough to control your anger instead of letting it control you.

The following sentences are all related thematically. They express a wide difference of opinions and attitudes. You may agree with some of them and disagree with others. Please discuss what you think the sentences mean and what you think about them.

5

Self-control is the ability to carry a credit card and not abuse it.

6

At no time is self-control more difficult than in times of success.

7

How can a man control his destiny when he can't control himself?

8

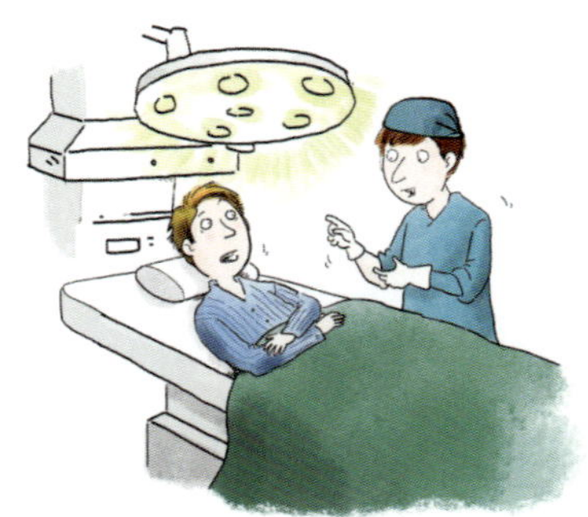

Man cannot remake himself without suffering, being both marble and sculptor.

1

— We're going to crash! Let's get out of here!
— But we don't have parachutes.
— We'll die if we stay aboard.
— We'll die if we jump.
— But at least we'll die trying.

2

Officer, I was desperate*. So I took a wrong turn with my life.

We're not here to discuss your traffic violations.

desperate : willing to do anything to change a very bad situation, and not caring about danger

3

– Being a burglar means a good, steady income. But I hate the hours!
– I'm watching a burglar at work. Please take notes!
– Why? Are you going to turn him in* to the police?
– No. I'm going to change professions.

turn (sb) in : give control of (sb) to the police

4

stand for (sth) : allow or accept (sth)
revenge : (sth) you do in order to punish (sb) who has harmed or offended you

5

- Aren't you hungry?
- No, I'm all right.
- No money?
- Well, now that you mention it, I left my credit card at home.
- I'll buy! What would you like?
- What's the limit on your card?

6

I used to be rich, but I spent all my money foolishly. I guess I didn't have any self-control. How about you?

I don't know. I never had any opportunity to find out.

7

Maybe you've had enough.
No. Absolutely not. "Enough" happened an hour ago.
RUM

Don't worry. I'm well-protected.
I hope this isn't going to hurt.

ISSUE 25
Is Life Fair?

Of course life is not fair! The universe has no moral sense. Everything is mechanical* and ordered in a random* way. Bad things happen to good people, and good things happen to bad people. And sometimes people get what they deserve (from a human standpoint). For example, I may get hit by a truck and killed this afternoon while I am visiting my sick friend in the hospital. However, having said that, it is still possible to arrange* our lives in a way that will tend to let us benefit from good decisions. I can't stop the truck driver from hitting me, but I can obey traffic rules and wear my seat belt and have good medical insurance and thus maybe avoid death or serious injury or the destruction of my lifestyle if I survive. But most of the time, we tempt fate*. We routinely do stupid, senseless things that eventually catch up with* us. We seem to enjoy playing Russian roulette* with our lives, and then when we pull the trigger* on a chamber* that isn't empty we get mad and say, "Life is not fair!"

All these stars and galaxies out there! It's hard to imagine that there isn't intelligent life out there. But, then again, sometimes it's hard to imagine that there's intelligent life here, too.

---

mechanical : relating to physical energy and forces **random :** happening, appearing, or chosen without any definite plan, aim, or pattern **arrange :** organize the details of (sth) before it happens; plan (sth)
tempt fate : do (sth) that is very risky or dangerous **catch up with :** begin to have a damaging effect on
Russian roulette : dangerous game in which people fire a gun with a single bullet at their heads without knowing if the bullet will be shot or not **pull the trigger :** shoot or fire
chamber : part of the barrel that receives the charge

Comprehension

1. What is the nature of the universe?
2. Are we entirely at the mercy of* arbitrary*, random events?
3. What does "playing Russian roulette with our lives" mean?

Express  Yourself

1. In your case, do you think life has been fair?
2. Is life worth living, even if it is grossly* unfair?
3. What determines the "fairness" of any given situation?
4. If we are in an unfair environment, can we free ourselves from it? How?
5. If life is not fair, who is responsible?
6. What do poor people complain most about?
7. What do rich people complain most about?
8. If the poor got what they wanted, would it be unfair to the rich? And vice versa*?
9. What do young people complain most about?
10. What do parents complain most about?
11. What do teachers complain most about?
12. What do husbands complain about?
13. What do wives complain about?
14. What do workers complain about?
15. What do bosses complain about?
16. Some people joke, "The rich are declared innocent while the poor are found guilty regardless* of the evidence or circumstances." Do you believe this claim? Do you think people are equally treated by the law? Why or why not?

---

at the mercy of : completely in the power or under the control of
arbitrary : not planned or chosen for a particular reason
grossly : in a way that is very obvious or noticeable
vice versa : the opposite of a statement is also true
regardless of : without being stopped or affected by (sth)

More Talking Points

Are the following conditions fair or unfair? Why?

1. Poor people suffer from famines*, even though the rich still eat.
2. Most countries are dictatorships*, and only a few are democracies.
3. Ex-convicts are never reprieved* from their past, even if they have reformed*.
4. Bright students without money can't continue their education.
5. The already-rich make more money than the have-nots, and they also pay less in taxes.
6. Gorgeous* people make more money, get promoted faster, and have more socially desirable marriages than plain* people.
7. The handicapped have difficulty finding suitable jobs, even in areas where their disability is irrelevant*.
8. Everyone pays the same sales tax regardless of means*.
9. Women are not conscripted*.
10. Married women are treated worse by their employers than men or single women are.
11. Large deposits* get better returns* in a bank than small ones.
12. Students from a rich family receive scholarships simply because they show better scholastic performance.
13. Smokers are prohibited from smoking in their own apartment.
14. Speed limits are imposed equally on all drivers regardless of their driving skills.
15. Healthy people who seldom visit hospitals pay the same insurance premiums as sick people who must have multiple medical treatments.
16. Retirement age is fixed by law regardless of an individual's working ability.
17. Childless couples pay higher taxes than couples with kids.
18. Elderly people over age 65 use subways free of charge. (This policy hurts revenues causing fare hikes for everyone.)
19. Career women are still pressured to do more domestic chores than their husbands.
20. Expensive cars require the same property taxes as the less expensive ones.

---

famine : situation in which a large number of people have little or no food for a long time and many people die
dictatorship : rule, control, or leadership by one person with total power
reprieve : bring relief to
reform : change your behavior and become a better person
gorgeous : very beautiful or attractive
plain : not handsome or beautiful
irrelevant : not useful in or not relating to a particular situation, and therefore not important
means : money or income that you have
conscript : force (sb) to serve in the armed forces
deposit : amount of money that is put in a bank account
returns : amount of profit from an investment

Opinion Samples

1. Fairness is always a subjective* matter. I recall a story about Jan Smuts, the South African statesman. He was once asked to arbitrate* an inheritance dispute between two brothers. He immediately adopted an overly* friendly and accommodating* attitude toward one of the brothers and an indifferent* aspect toward the other. After hearing both sides of the case, and encouraging the friendly one, he drew up* a plan to divide the assets. The friendly brother would get A, B, and C, while the other one would get D, E. and F. Smuts asked the friendly brother if he thought that was a fair settlement. The brother looked it over and agreed that, yes, it was quite satisfactory. So Smuts said, "Good. Since you agree that it is fair and equitable*, then you won't mind if you get D, E, and F, while your brother gets A, B. and C." I can't think of a better example of actual fairness.

2. Rich celebrities and important people get a lot of freebies*. People take them out to eat, they give them expensive gifts, and they treat them to vacations and various luxuries, even though they are quite capable of paying for these things themselves. However, ordinary people must usually pay full price for whatever they get, even for things they need just to survive, although doing so may constitute* a severe economic burden*. The more people have, the more they get, while those with less cannot expect to get anything at all. Is that fair?

subjective : based on feelings or opinions rather than facts
arbitrate : settle an argument between two people or groups after hearing the opinions and ideas of both
overly : to an excessive degree; too
accommodating : willing to do what (sb) else wants or requests
indifferent : not interested in or concerned about (sth)
draw (sth) up : prepare a plan, proposal, agreement, or other document in detail
equitable : fair and impartial
freebie : (sth) that is given for free
constitute : create
burden : source of great worry or stress

Unfair from Birth

Tanya : I do so look forward* to having a baby!

Gary : Babies are symbols of possibility, you know. They represent the future and the hope that it will be better than the present.

Tanya : That's a very philosophical attitude.

Gary : But unfortunately, symbols are not emblematic* of reality. The future will continue to be pretty much like the present.

Tanya : You're such a pessimist! I know that my baby will have everything good in life, and I plan to do all in my power to make it so.

Gary : Yes, of course you will. But, no matter how special your child is, or how great a mother you are, the odds* are never evenly* distributed. Some children are always going to be advantaged over others.

Tanya : I guess you mean that rich families can give their offspring the best available opportunities. Schooling, a prestigious family name, contacts*, capital*, that sort of thing.

Gary : That's part of what I mean. But all those advantages can be countered* through planning, perseverance, and good luck. What I'm really talking about are the genetic advantages some children have, and most don't.

Tanya : What do you mean?

Gary : Almost everyone falls* within a fairly narrow IQ range.

Tanya : Yes. I remember that from my psychology class.

Gary : But there's a bell-shaped curve for intelligence. On both sides of the vast middle there are a few unfortunates who are not intelligent at all and a few geniuses.

Tanya : OK. But what's your point?

Gary : Obviously, the geniuses have a huge advantage over everyone else, and everyone else has a huge advantage over the low-IQ ones. But this characteristic is not something that can be overcome through diligence; it's a permanent state of affairs.

Tanya : But almost everyone has "normal" intelligence. That's good enough to lead a decent, productive life.

Gary : Maybe so, but the statistically unusual ones are unduly* rewarded or punished through no action of their own.

---

look forward to (sth) : expect (sth) with pleasure   emblematic : seeming to represent or be a sign of (sth)
the odds : the chances or likelihood of (sth) happening or being the case   evenly : equally
contact : (sb) you know who can be helpful to you, esp. in business
capital : money or property, esp. when it is used to start a business or to produce more wealth
countered : balanced   fall : belong in a particular category or range
unduly : to an extreme, unreasonable, or unnecessary degree; excessively

Tanya : That's not fair, but that's just the way it is.

Gary : And it extends across the whole spectrum* of human attributes*. Some are born to become beautiful adults, and they will have many opportunities thrust upon* them that won't be as readily available to ugly people or even ordinary, plain folks.

Tanya : My husband and I both look okay. Our kid will probably be all right.

Gary : "All right" is just not competitive, though. I'm not just talking about becoming a rich and famous model or actor; it's true across the board* that gorgeous people have more success than others.

Tanya : I felt a lot better about having a baby before I talked to you.

Gary : And it's the same for everything. Some are born with musical talent or athletic ability, and most aren't. It's clear that even personality is largely determined at birth rather than developed through life.

Tanya : Despite all you say, I'm excited about becoming a mother, and I know my child will turn out* special. So, don't talk to me about it anymore.

QUESTIONS

1. What if all humans had exactly the same traits*? Would that be a good or bad thing?
2. If a genius were also ugly and unsocial, would those characteristics tend to nullify* the advantages of intelligence?
3. We all know about people with enormous disadvantages who accomplish incredible achievements. Do their experiences entirely negate* Gary's point?

---

spectrum : range attribute : usually good quality or feature that (sb/sth) has
thrust on/upon : force (sb) to have or accept (sth)
across the board : affecting or including all people, classes, or categories
turn out : happen, end, or develop in a particular way trait : particular quality in (sb's) character
nullify : prevent (sth) from having any effect negate : make ineffective; nullify

Read & Discuss

Who or What Is to Blame?

Poverty is a fact in human history. In part, this is a relative notion, at least in most societies that are not based on economic equality. A poor person in one place might be regarded as rather well-off in others; for instance, in a rich society, even poor people might have a car or a TV or a place to live and an adequate diet. In part, poverty is a matter of perception; I grew up in a family that had almost no money, but we never thought we were poor. However, absolute poverty, by any standard or definition of the term, certainly does exist everywhere, in circumstances where people cannot live long, healthy lives, where starvation or malnutrition is pervasive*, where disease is prevalent*. Who is responsible for this state of human disaster? Some people want to blame the individuals for their want* of ability, ambition, or expectation. Some want to blame the government for not establishing effective programs to provide the basic necessities for decent* human lifestyles. Others want to blame society, or culture itself, for brainwashing* its members (or a designated portion thereof) into accepting those conditions as being normal and proper.

QUESTIONS

1. Do most poor people have the resources needed to improve their condition to any considerable degree?
2. In your culture, are there any attitudes or institutions* that tend to prevent people from improving their situation?
3. Does your government go far enough (or too far?) in providing decent lives for poor people?

---

pervasive : existing in every part of (sth) **prevalent :** common or widespread **want :** lack
decent : acceptable or good enough **brainwash :** make (sb) adopt radically different beliefs by using systematic and often forcible pressure **handout :** money or goods that are given to (sb), for example because they are poor **institution :** custom, practice, or law that is accepted and used by many people

Let's Talk Funny

If God Is Responsible for Hunger, Is He Also To Blame for Obesity*?

Man: God cannot exist! At least, not a moral God!

Friend: What do you mean by that?

Man: Obesity has become a big issue in rich nations, but in poor countries people can't even feed themselves. How could this happen if God existed?

Friend: Oh, God definitely* exists! But he wants us all to understand that life is unfair and we need to rely on his mercy* to survive

QUESTIONS

1. Is God responsible for man-made human misfortune?
2. Do religious teachings ever help perpetuate* human misfortune?
3. Would solving the obesity problem also relieve* world hunger? Or are they unrelated?

---

obesity : condition of being very fat in a way that is dangerous to your health
definitely : without doubt
mercy : compassion or forgiveness
perpetuate : make a situation, attitude etc., esp. a bad one, continue to exist
relieve : make (a problem) less serious

Points to Ponder

1

I know the world isn't fair, but why isn't it ever unfair in my favor*?

2

Sometimes on the way to accomplishing a dream, people get lost and find a better one.

3

Success is where preparation and opportunity meet.

4

You can't do anything about the length of your life, but you can do something about its width and depth.

---

in (sb's) favor : in support of (sb); in a way that helps or benefit (sb)

The following sentences are all related thematically. They express a wide difference of opinions and attitudes. You may agree with some of them and disagree with others. Please discuss what you think the sentences mean and what you think about them.

5

The art of living lies not in eliminating* troubles but in growing through them.

6

Live your life so that you won't be afraid of having your phone tapped*.

7

Life is tragic for those who have plenty to live on but nothing to live for.

8

Man has learned to fly like a bird and swim like a fish, when all he needs is to learn to live like a MAN.

eliminate : completely get rid of (sth) that is unnecessary or unwanted
tapped : connected so that conversation can be listened to secretly

1

2

Let's go around the forest.

It's too far. Let's stop here.

Look, you two, let's go straight ahead. We can't get lost as long as we head in the right direction.

3

PREPARATION

OPPORTUNITY

I always expected opportunity to come my way. But I was afraid I'd miss it if I didn't pay attention. So I didn't want to be distracted* by concentrating on prep.

I've been preparing for a long time, but I never thought I'd get my chance.

distracted : unable to think about or pay attention to (sth); unable to concentrate

4

– How do these hospitals continue to exist? They have no patients!
– Everybody wants a longer life.
– Nobody is interested in a broader one.
– Or a deeper one.
– But this line is so long, by the time we get in we'll already be too old.
– Actually, I'd like to have a broader AND a deeper life. But my insurance won't cover* it.

cover : pay for

5

We have a bridge over the Sea of Trouble now. Why is that man still rowing a boat

You have a car and a bridge. But there aren't any gas stations!

6

I'm in the dog house because someone overheard* my private conversations.

I'm very comfortable knowing that I never had to worry about honest barking.

overhear : accidentally hear what other people are saying, when they do not know that you have heard

7

8

torn : unable to decide what to do stumped : at a loss; unable to work out what to do or say

ISSUE 26

Crime & Punishment

The nation's per capita* income has steadily grown, and educational opportunities have expanded, but its crime rate has also increased. In particular, juvenile delinquency* is growing rapidly. If conditions are improving, why isn't criminality on the decline? Furthermore, not only is the crime itself costly to society, but so is its punishment. It not only destroys individual lives but entire families, and the bill for incarceration* is also expensive; many taxpayers complain that their money is being used to support "welfare for lawbreakers."

What is the key factor in criminality? Genetics? Family problems? Social alienation*? Peer pressure? Cultural upheaval* caused by the switchover* from a traditional to a modern society? Lax*, permissive societal norms? Drugs and/or alcohol? Lack of individual conscience and responsibility? The glorification of violence in the media? The phenomenon of copycat crimes*? Perhaps all of the above? So, while the cause of criminality is still inexplicable*, the cure is necessarily even more so. Is better education the answer? Harsher punishment? More intrusive* social intervention? A return to traditional values? Censorship*?

---

per capita : in relation to people taken individually **juvenile delinquency :** criminal acts or offenses by young people **incarcerate :** put (sb) in prison **alienate :** cause (sb) to feel that they no longer belong in a particular group, society, etc. **upheaval :** major change that causes a lot of conflict, confusion, etc.
switchover : instance of adopting a new policy, position, way of life, etc. **lax :** not strict enough
copycat crime : crime that is similar to a famous crime done by another person **inexplicable :** not able to be explained or understood **intrusive :** affecting (sb's) life or interrupting them in an unwanted and annoying way
censorship : practice of officially examining books, movies, etc., and suppressing unacceptable parts
mandatory : required by law or rules; compulsory **at one's leisure :** at one's ease or convenience

Comprehension

1. Why is crime on the rise*?
2. What can be done to reverse* the trend?
3. What does "social alienation" mean?

Express  Yourself

1. What causes people to commit crimes?
2. Define criminality. How can it be reduced?
3. Have you ever broken the law? If so, what were the circumstances?
4. Why is juvenile delinquency on the rise? Or, is it really?
5. Are laws too harsh or too permissive?
6. Do you think the punishment of a first-time offender should usually be commuted*? What do you think about penalizing* ex-convicts more severely?
7. Should parents be responsible for their children's actions?
8. In what way (if any) is society responsible for criminality?
9. What is the most effective deterrent* to heinous* acts?
10. Should we use taxpayers' money to feed, house, and clothe criminals, and also to give them medical treatment and educational/vocational opportunities?
11. Do you think most law-enforcement professionals are well trained, honest, and competent?
12. How can we help ex-convicts successfully adapt* to social values? Should we?
13. Do you think adultery* should be punishable by law? Or should it be a matter to be settled among the relevant individuals?
14. What do you think about severely fining* wealthy miscreants* instead of jailing them?
15. If an accused criminal pleads not guilty by reason of insanity*, can you buy* that as a reason to excuse* the crime?
16. If someone killed a burglar who broke into his house, should he be excused as a matter of self-defense or be punished for murder?
17. Do you think the statute of limitations* should be abolished for certain crimes? For which ones? And why?

---

on the rise : increasing in amount, number, level, etc. reverse : changing (sth) to an opposite state or condition commute : change (a punishment) to a less severe one penalize : punish (sb) for breaking a rule or law deterrent : (sth) that makes (sb) decide not to do (sth) heinous : very bad or evil adapt : change your behavior so that it is easier to live in a particular place or situation adultery : sex between a married person and (sb) who is not their wife or husband fine : make (sb) pay money as a punishment miscreant : (sb) who does (sth) illegal or morally wrong insanity : severe mental illness buy : accept or believe (sth) as true excuse : be an acceptable reason for (sth); justify statute of limitations : law setting a time limit on legal action in certain cases

More Talking Points

Briefly define the following crimes and their most appropriate punishments:

1. DWI (driving while intoxicated)
2. Bribery
3. Defamation* of character (libel*, slander*)
4. Forgery*
5. Fraud
6. Robbery
7. Rape (including date rape and marital rape)
8. Shoplifting
9. Mugging*
10. Murder
11. Sexual harassment
12. Stalking*
13. Prostitution
14. Vandalism*
15. Drug dealing
16. Perjury*
17. Terrorism
18. Littering
19. Gambling
20. Tax evasion
21. Child molestation
22. Polygamy
23. Arson*
24. Graffiti*
25. Human trafficking*
26. Burglary
27. Extortion*
28. Kidnapping
29. Pornography
30. Treason*
31. Torture
32. Cruelty to animals
33. Obstruction of justice*
34. Hit-and-run*
35. Sexting
36. Identity theft
37. Pickpocketing
38. Hacking
39. Video voyeurism*
40. Public nakedness

---

defamation : act of saying false things in order to make people have a bad opinion of (sb/sth)
libel : act of publishing a false statement that causes people to have a bad opinion of (sb)
slander : act of making a false spoken statement that causes people to have a bad opinion of (sb)
forgery : crime of falsely making or copying a document in order to deceive people
mugging : act of attacking and robbing (sb)
stalking : crime of following and watching (sb) over a long period of time, in a way that is annoying or threatening
vandalism : act of deliberately destroying or damaging property
perjury : crime of telling a lie in a court of law after promising to tell the truth
arson : crime of deliberately setting fire to property
graffiti : writing and pictures illegally drawn on the walls of buildings, trains, etc.
human trafficking : crime of trading in human beings for the purpose of exploitation
extortion : crime of getting money from (sb) by the use of force or threats
treason : crime of being disloyal to your country or its government, esp. by helping its enemies or trying to remove the government using violence
obstruction of justice : crime of trying to stop police from learning the truth about (sth)
hit-and-run : crime of causing a motor vehicle accident and then running away without helping the injured or informing police
video voyeurism : act of secretly recording (sb) in an intimate situation, such as when they are dressing or undressing

Opinion Samples

1. Just as in child rearing, the question is not (usually — extreme cases may be the exception) whether punishment is too harsh or too lenient*. The question is: Is it fairly and predictably applied? There should be no guesswork*. If a ten-year-old boy, or a burglar, has committed an impermissible act, that boy or that burglar should know that he will be punished and what that punishment will precisely entail*. His younger brother, or his sister, or another burglar, should not be treated differently, and if he repeats his offense he should be punished in the same way. This will not completely deter* all bad acts by ten-year-old boys or by burglars, but it will give them pause* to reconsider before going ahead, and in some cases they will decide that the risk outweighs* the perceived benefits.

2. We are not independent actors, isolated from society, in complete control over every activity and attitude. We are influenced in our judgment and behavior by our peers, our parents, our role models, our colleagues, our neighbors. We read books and magazines, we watch movies and TV shows, we play video games and use social media. We are bombarded* with ads, commercials, and propaganda*. We are part of an all-enveloping* culture that is impressed* upon us from infancy via folk beliefs, religious injunctions*, educational systems, and social norms. So how can we possibly think that "society" has "no responsibility" for criminality? Society is at the very least an enabler and an accomplice* in all that we say or do.

lenient : not harsh, severe, or strict
guesswork : act or process of finding an answer by guessing
entail : involve (sth) as a necessary or inevitable part or consequence
deter : prevent (sth) from happening
pause : temporary stop
outweigh : be more important or valuable than (sth) else
bombarded : inundated; overwhelmed
propaganda : ideas or statements that are often false or exaggerated and that are spread in order to help a cause, a political leader, a government, etc.
envelop : completely enclose or surround (sth)
impress : put (sth) in (sb's) mind
injunction : authoritative warning or order
accomplice : (sb) who helps another commit a crime

Getting Away with* It

Myrtle: Did you hear the news?

Joe : What news?

Myrtle: About that CEO who stabbed* his young girlfriend to death?

Joe : Yeah? What about him?

Myrtle: He was found guilty but only sentenced to one year in prison due to all the charitable good work he and his company have been involved in!

Joe : No! It can't be!

Myrtle: No. It's true. See for yourself*.

Joe : If that had been me, I'd have gotten at least a life sentence. Maybe I'd even face execution.

Myrtle: But, obviously, your biggest crime is that you're not rich.

Joe : That's a fact! If I had money, I could get away with anything.

Myrtle: The real surprise is that he was even found guilty at all. If he hadn't been too stingy to hire a better lawyer, he probably would have been found innocent.

Joe : Maybe there were extenuating circumstances*. Maybe his girlfriend had done something to enrage him.

Myrtle: You enrage me on a constant basis, but that doesn't mean I have a right to kill you, does it?

Joe : I hope not. And, for your sake, it doesn't give me the right to kill you, either. Though, sometimes.....

Myrtle: This is nothing to joke about! We should never blame the victim and let the victimizer get off*.

Joe : You're right. I apologize.

Myrtle: There's something seriously wrong with a system of justice that routinely lets guilty rich people avoid punishment while throwing maximum sentences at poor people for the same crime!

Joe : Maybe poor people do commit more crimes. Maybe their poverty and lack of education and lack of opportunity cause them to disregard* the law more often.

Myrtle: Poor people have the same sense of morality and decency as rich ones do — maybe even more so, since the rich ones seem to think they will get away with their crimes if they're ever caught

Joe : That's just an opinion. The opposite might also be true.

---

get away with : avoid being caught; escape stab : wound (sb) with a pointed weapon (such as a knife) see for yourself : look at (sth) so that you can find out if it is true extenuating circumstances : facts about a situation which make a wrong or illegal action easier to understand or excuse get off : get little or no punishment for a crime disregard : ignore (sth) or treat (sth) as unimportant

Myrtle: Just for the sake of argument, let's suppose that the poor are more likely to engage in criminal activity. I don't think that's the case, but let's just say so for now.

Joe : OK. Proceed*.

Myrtle: Even if only the one rich guy killed his girlfriend and if a thousand poor people killed theirs, the poor murderers would all most likely be given the maximum sentence, and the rich one would hardly be punished at all. That's a travesty* of justice!

Joe : The same thing can be said about celebrities — they're much less likely to be convicted or given heavy punishment. I agree that's a problem. But the real lesson is: Don't commit the crime and you needn't worry about the punishment.

Myrtle: Unfortunately, even that is not true. Poor people are also much more likely to be arrested, tried, and convicted of crimes that they didn't commit.

P1: Stop! Or we'll shoot.
R1: Quick! Throw out all the money to distract the police so we can get away.
P1: Grab the cash.
P2: But the crooks will get away.
P1: So what? The system will just release them anyway.
R2: Whew! That was a close one.
R1: But after all that hard work, we don't have a thing to show for it.
R2: The cops can't put that money in the bank without getting in trouble. So we'll just steal it back from them in a few days.

QUESTIONS

1. Have you ever had to go to court as part of some criminal case, perhaps a traffic accident or divorce or lawsuit? How would you describe the proceedings?
2. Wealthy defendants can afford better lawyers than poor ones and in general have more resources they can employ*, including social contacts and public reputations. Is it unfair for them to use their advantages in their own behalf? Should they be forced to handicap* their own cases?
3. What is your plan to engineer* a perfectly fair system of justice?

---

proceed : continue travesty : extremely bad example of (sth)
employ : make use of handicap : make success or progress difficult for (sb)
engineer : produce or plan (sth) esp. in a clever and skillful way

Read & Discuss

Capital Punishment*

Capital punishment is becoming increasingly rare in today's world, though once it was quite common. Advocates* have always relied on arguments centered on morality and deterrence to justify the practice, while opponents have posed a very different set of moral values and have challenged the very existence of any deterrent effect. Economics has also become part of the equation*, with proponents claiming that executions are far less expensive than prolonged incarceration, while opponents insist that the opposite is actually true. On both sides of the issue, people tend to have very strong feelings and find it difficult to understand or appreciate* the counterarguments*. So I put it to you: Does the state have a right (or duty) to take the life of an individual? If so, under what circumstances and for what crimes? Is there any reason to try to make executions painless and "humane"*? And what can be done about the executions of innocent people?

— I'm innocent.
— That's what they all say.
— But it's true. If you kill an innocent man, won't your conscience bother you?
— You should thank me. We all die someday. The only difference is that you know the exact moment it will happen, so I have eliminated* all the guesswork.

QUESTIONS

1. What is the moral argument in favor of capital punishment? The moral argument against it?
2. Which is worse, spending one's life in prison or being executed?
3. "The punishment should fit* the crime." For example: Do you think it should apply to the death penalty?

---

capital punishment : punishment by death advocate : (sb) who argues for or supports a cause or policy
equation : situation or problem in which several factors must be taken into account
appreciate : recognize the full implications of (sth) counterargument : argument in opposition to another
humane : characterized by kindness, mercy, or compassion eliminate : remove (sth) that is not wanted or needed; get rid of (sth) fit : be suitable or appropriate for (sb/sth)

Let's Talk Funny

Art Dealer Admits Selling a Fake* Picasso

Judge: You are charged with* making money by selling a fake Picasso. How do you plead*?

Accused dealer: Guilty but not guilty, Your Honor.

Judge: Why not?

Accused dealer: I sold a phony* Picasso to a crook*, but he paid for it in counterfeit* money.

– I swear* this is a real Picasso. It's priceless*. So you're getting a real bargain* at this price.
– How do I know it's real?
– He signed it right here. See?
– Okay, I guess so. Do you take credit cards?
– For stolen goods? Are you kidding? Cash only.
– Well, all right. Count it.
– How do I know it's real?
– It's got the treasurer's signature on it. Right here.

I've caught you both red-handed*. I don't know if the painting is real or not, but I never understood why anyone would pay a fortune for modern art. My six-year-old son can paint better than that.

QUESTIONS

1. Does one need to profit from wrongdoing in order to commit a crime?
2. Do people need to know they are breaking the law in order to be convicted*?
3. If you buy an expensive object at a fraction* of its genuine value and you believe it to have been stolen, are you just as guilty as the thief? Or have you merely taken advantage of a good deal?

---

fake : not true or real **charged with :** accused of **plead :** say in court that you are either guilty or not guilty of a crime **phony :** not true, real, or genuine **crook :** dishonest person or criminal **counterfeit :** made to look like an exact copy of (sth) in order to trick people **swear :** state (sth) very strongly and sincerely **priceless :** so precious that its value cannot be determined **bargain :** thing bought or offered for sale more cheaply than is usual or expected **red-handed :** while doing (sth) wrong or illegal **convict :** declare (sb) to be guilty of a criminal offense **fraction :** very small amount of (sth)

Points to Ponder

1

The common argument that crime is caused by poverty is a slander* against the poor.

2

We can't stop crime, so why not legalize it and then tax it out of business?

3

Every single person in jail for a violent crime had a nightmare of a childhood.

4

The cure for crime is not the electric chair, but the high chair.

---

slander : false and malicious spoken statement

The following sentences are all related thematically. They express a wide difference of opinions and attitudes. You may agree with some of them and disagree with others. Please discuss what you think the sentences mean and what you think about them.

5

The biggest accomplice to the crime of corruption* is our own indifference*.

6

There is no bigger crime than thinking you are right, no matter what.

Surveillance* cameras might reduce crime but no studies show that they result in greater happiness of everyone involved.

Insider trading is a serious crime with an easy solution: Always trade outside.

---

corruption : dishonest or illegal behavior, esp. by powerful people (such as government officials or police officers) **indifference :** lack of interest in or concern about (sth) **surveillance :** act of carefully watching (sb/sth), esp. in order to prevent or detect a crime

1

– Why do you pick on* me? I didn't do it. It's no crime to be poor.
– But being poor gives you an incentive to break the law. If I were poor, I'd be willing to take desperate measures too in order to feed myself and my family.
– Nonetheless, Officer, believe it or not, I'm an honest man. Maybe if I were less honest I wouldn't be so poor.

– What do you think, Sir? Do you believe him? Lock him up and throw away the key! Not because he's a criminal or even dishonest, but because he's stupid.
– Stupid?
– Of course! Most crimes are committed by rich people, but they're smart enough, and rich enough, to get away with it. After all, the rich are the best criminals because we're most likely not to get punished. But poor people are routinely punished whether or not they're guilty.

pick on (sb) : single (sb) out for blame or criticism unfairly

2

– I've lost complete faith in the government!
– Me, too.
– First they cut into* our rackets* by legalizing gambling, prostitution, and other sins.
– Just so they can tax those industries.
– They claim they will tax them out of existence, but all they'll really do is keep them in business in order to raise revenues.
– But meanwhile, they're putting the honest mom-and-pop-store* criminals like us out of business.
– What are we to do?
– Maybe we should raise the ante* and go big-time*. Kidnapping, murder-for-hire*, that sort of thing.
– That's pretty dangerous.
– Yes, but we have to change with the times if we want to make a living.
– I don't know. The government will probably just get a monopoly over those activities too. And then what will we do?
– Get a government job, I guess.
– No, they're bigger crooks than we are.

cut into : take (sb) else's position or role **racket :** business that makes money through illegal activities
mom-and-pop stores : stores owned by and run by a married couple or by a small number of people
raise the ante : increase what is at stake **big-time :** in a big way
murder-for-hire : crime of killing (sb) because you have been paid to do it

3

I sentence you to 20 years at hard labor.

Do you guys memorize a script? I hear the same story every day.

But, Your Honor, I never had a chance. My parents were alcoholics and couldn't keep a job. I was abused from the age of five. I never had any good role models, so I didn't know right from wrong. But now I realize the error of my ways and want to reform.

4

– We must take care, and, from an early age, make sure that our son knows the difference between right and wrong.
– That's right. That's the only way to make sure he becomes an honest citizen instead of a criminal. Moral training begins and ends at home, with the parents.
– The teaching must begin in the high chair, or else the electric chair is inevitable*.

I can tell already that they'll never let me have any fun.

They never gave me any high chair. Does that mean I'm doomed* to lead a criminal life?

inevitable : impossible to avoid doomed : destined

5

root out : find and get rid of

6

– Whatever I did, I did it because it was the right thing to do. No one should be punished for following his own code of conduct*.
– Some codes of conduct justify any crime. They are self-serving* and take no cognizance of* social norms.
– I admit that I killed 47 people, but they were all bad men. They all deserved to die.
– Maybe so. But nobody gave you the authority to act as judge, jury, and executioner. They never had a fair trial before an impartial judge.
– I never had a jury of my peers. None of them were killers.

code of conduct : rules or principles of (sb's) behavior on a particular occasion **self-serving :** showing concern only about your own needs and interests **take cognizance of :** give attention to

7

I know I'm being watched all the time, so I'm afraid to do anything. If I say something that is politically incorrect, I might get in trouble. If I get angry or drink too much, there might be repercussions* against me. If I accidently say something bad about my wife or boss or the police, I might have to face the consequences. I guess I'm "safe," but I am sure not happy.

repercussion : unintended consequence occurring some time after an event or action, esp. an unwelcome one

– Senator Brown, I just want to let you know how this bill I'm working on will affect pharmaceutical prices if it passes. Just so you'll be prepared to act.

– Thank you very much, Senator Smith. I'll keep you posted* on that highway bill that my committee is drafting*.

– The public always complains that we're too partisan* and can never cooperate if we're in different parties.

– Yes, that's too bad. They completely misunderstand how it really works.

keep (sb) posted : regularly tell (sb) the most recent news about (sth)
draft : prepare a preliminary version of **partisan :** strongly supporting one particular party

ISSUE 27

Social Pressure

An age-old* question is where to draw the line between Me and Everyone Else. Humans are, on the one hand, self-conscious individuals, and social animals on the other. A part of us wants to have every wish gratified immediately, no matter what it is. Another part of us feels obligated* to compromise* with the needs and attitudes of other people (including those we have never met who belong to some extended group we belong to) and even to sacrifice our own desires and sometimes our lives (not only for close relatives but also in defense of an abstract* ideal). Individuals vary* in their capacity for altruism*, as do cultures — some are highly group-conscious, and others not so much. But the dilemma* remains the same for each of us: Do I do what I want to do or what society expects me to do?

I'm a slave to a schedule imposed on me by invisible bosses. Someone tells me what time I'm supposed to be at work, what time I'll leave, when I'll eat, what tasks I have to perform there, how to do them, what to wear, who to talk to. Sometimes I wish I had control over my own destiny and could do as I pleased.

I'm as free as a bird, and as broke. I absolutely do whatever I want to do, whenever I wish, as long as it doesn't cost any money. I have lots of casual friends who envy my independence, but it's hard to have any enduring* relationships when I don't have any stability in life. Freedom isn't free.

Which is better for me?

---

age-old : very old; having existed for a very long time
obligated : made to do (sth) because it is the law, duty, or the right thing
compromise : give up (sth) you want in order to reach an agreement
abstract : based on general ideas or principles rather than specific examples or real events
vary : be different **altruism :** practice of thinking of the needs and desires of other people instead of your own
dilemma : situation in which you have to make a difficult choice
enduring : continuing to exist for a long time, esp. in spite of difficulties; lasting

Comprehension

1. In what way is the human personality split*, according to the article?
2. In what ways are we motivated by individual preferences*?
3. In what ways are we motivated by peer pressure?

Express Yourself

1. Teens are pressured by their parents to be all-A students. What happens if they don't live up to* these expectations?
2. Does everybody feel pressured to get a college diploma? Why?
3. Adults often look for well-paid jobs instead of doing what they are really interested in. Which do you think is more important? Why?
4. Most people seem preoccupied* with improving their appearance rather than enriching* their mind. Is that a worthwhile choice? Why or why not?
5. Do grownups feel pushed to "tie the knot"*? Why or why not?
6. Are married couples under pressure to have children? Should they be?
7. Does society put extra responsibility on the eldest son? Is that fair?
8. Do you think the husband and wife should share responsibility for finances? Or should it primarily be the job of one of them? Which one?
9. These days married people are pressured to be excellent spouses and parents, as well as to stay healthy, have good jobs, and be supportive children to their own parents simultaneously*. Do you think they can successfully juggle* all these demanding* roles?
10. Do you think cosmetic surgery is a result of social pressure? Why or why not?
11. What are the effects of social pressures on people who don't cope* well with them?
12. Is it possible to be completely free from all social pressure? Would that be desirable?

---

split : divided preference : greater liking for one alternative over another or others
live up to : do what is required by
preoccupied : thinking about (sth) a lot or too much
enrich : improve or enhance the quality or value
tie the knot : get married simultaneously : at the same time
juggle : try to fit two or more jobs, activities, etc. into your life, esp. when this is difficult
demanding : requiring much time, attention, or effort
cope with : deal with problems and difficult situations and try to come up with solutions

Opinion Samples

1. Almost everyone fights a losing battle with their own looks. The sad fact is that we reach our peak in terms of beauty during our adolescence and early adulthood. After that, our hair and teeth start to fall out*, our eyesight dims, our skin loses its freshness and elasticity*, we start to get wrinkled and overweight. We try mightily to retain our youthful vitality through exercise, cosmetics, and fashion choices, but in the end we cannot win. Instead of wasting so much time, money, and energy on trying to improve our appearance, we would be much better off investing in improving our wisdom, our understanding, our knowledge, and our tolerance — qualities that truly enhance* our lives as we grow older.

2. Like everything else in terms of our behavior, selflessness is a genetic trait. Self-preservation is an obvious necessity for the survival of the species, and as an extension of that, the protection of our immediate gene pool. So, many animals exhibit strong defense mechanisms in terms of the offspring and the herd, even at the expense of* individual sacrifice. But humans tend to go much further in terms of social obligation than other animals. This is because there are actually two genetic forces at work*; one is natural selection (the steady adaptation to the environmental niche* that humans occupy), and the other (often overlooked*) is sexual selection. Females may need physically strong males for protection and food supply (greatly sublimated* in modern society), but they also want mates who will be pleasant to spend a lifetime with; and they also recognize that males who have the skill, intelligence, and charm necessary to rise* in society will probably be able to provide them with better lifestyle prospects as well as better progeny*.

Dialog

Superficial Pressure Leads to Cosmetic Surgery

Jacques : Why don't you do something about your nose?

Marie : What's wrong with my nose?

Jacques : I think it spoils an otherwise beautiful face. It just isn't symmetrical.

Marie : Most men say they like my nose. They say it distinguishes me from the herd of supermodel wannabes* and gives my face character.

Jacques : Ah, yes. Men will say anything to appease* a desirable* woman. But they are not sincere.

Marie : You are very cynical*.

Jacques : Yes. But I am also a man and know how men think and behave. I am being absolutely candid*.

---

fall out : become detached and drop out elasticity : ability of an object or material to return to its normal shape or size enhance : improve (sth) at the expense of : so as to cause harm to or neglect of
at work : having an effect or influence environmental niche : environmental conditions in which a particular animal, plant, etc. lives overlooked : not noticed sublimated : modified into a culturally higher or socially more acceptable activity rise : become more popular, successful, etc. progeny : child or descendant of (sb)
wannabe : (sb) who tries to look or act like (sb) else such as a famous person appease : make (sb) pleased or less angry by giving or saying (sth) desired desirable : worth having or seeking; sexually attractive
cynical : believing that people are motivated by self-interest; distrustful of human sincerity or integrity
candid : expressing opinions and feelings honestly and sincerely

Marie : So why do you think I need a nose job?

Jacques : There is a reason, you know, why the supermodels are so successful. They look like ordinary women want to look — and how men want their women to look.

Marie : Oh, these tastes change all the time. Look at the gorgeous ideal of the early movie starlets* — very different from today's standards. Go back to European oil paintings of beautiful women a few hundred years ago, and the differences are even greater.

Jacques : Yes, I know. And there are also cultural and class differences. Asians and Africans and Westerners have very different notions of female beauty. But it is all irrelevant.

Marie : And why is that?

Jacques : Because you live here and now, not in the past or in a faraway land. And the closer you come to the contemporary notion of how a beautiful woman should look, the better off you will be. Socially, professionally, and financially.

Marie : So I should give up my individual pride and subscribe* to the herd mentality*?

Jacques : I wouldn't state it in such crude* terms — but, yes, exactly. And we live in a time when it is possible, almost easy, for people to look any way they wish.

Marie : But I wish to look as I do. I see no need for plastic surgery.

Jacques : And that, of course, is your prerogative*. But you should think about it.

Marie : I should do as I'm told, just because you are a man?

Jacques : Only if you wish to please more men. And, by the way, it will also please more women as well.

Marie : Okay, I'll take it under advisement*. But I don't expect to change my mind.

Jacques : A mind is not like a door. Once it is open, it may change. But the door will always stay the same.

Marie : Why is it always up to the female to bend to the will of the male?

Jacques : Ah, that is not the case. The pragmatic man will also be a chameleon* in terms of what society wants.

Life is hard! Every day is a strain. But I'm determined to make it.

Once I got into proper shape, social pressure is easy to deal with. Life is just a series of ups and downs.

If I just sit here patiently, everything will take care of itself. Why bother?

QUESTIONS

1. Which is more important, being oneself or conforming* to a social standard? Defend your answer.
2. How much autonomy* do you think we actually have in terms of what we want? Is everything just a social construct*?
3. When you go on a date, or meet a client, or socialize with your boss — how much attention do you give to your appearance?

---

starlet : young movie actress **subscribe to :** agree with or support (an opinion, theory, etc.)
herd mentality : particular way of thinking a large group of people has **crude :** offensively coarse or rude
prerogative : right or privilege **take (sth) under advisement :** consider (sth) carefully
chameleon : (sb) who often changes his or her beliefs or behavior in order to please others or to succeed
conform to : obey or agree with **autonomy :** freedom from external control or influence; independence
social construct : idea that has been created and accepted by the people in a society

Read & Discuss

The Problem of Global Identity and Individual Consciousness

A growing problem, especially among teenage girls but also among other groups (adolescent males, adults of both genders) is the social despair* of not fitting a cookie-cutter* mold of how we're supposed to act, and especially how we're supposed to look. The ubiquitous* image-producing machinery of mass media — magazines, TV, movies, and cyber sites — is making us all acutely conscious of our failings in matching up to* "perfection" as it is presented to us. Other, less commercially viable* qualities we possess are undervalued. So, out of shame and frustration, we begin to isolate ourselves and become, of course, even more isolated as a result, and even more obsessed with the mass mediated* world. Cyber bullying further exposes and victimizes us. We are indeed social animals, and we need to feel like we are a valuable part of a wider society, and so our isolation leads us to more loneliness, more anxiety, and greater depression. The result may be a pronounced* suicidal tendency. And so, the great irony is that a technology that enables us to contact and communicate instantaneously with anyone and everyone in the world has had the perverse* effect of reducing our physical social interaction and heightening our egotistical* angst*.

QUESTIONS

1. Do you ever find yourself modeling yourself after some celebrity? Do you see other people doing that?
2. On the whole*, do you think social media improve your life or make it more complicated*?
3. What can we do to counter* the ill effects of mass mediation*?

---

despair : feeling of no longer having any hope **cookie-cutter :** very similar to other things of the same kind **ubiquitous :** present, appearing, or found everywhere **match up to :** be as good as or equal to **viable :** capable of being done or used; workable **mass mediated :** conveyed by mass media **pronounced :** very easy to notice **perverse :** contrary to the accepted or expected standard or practice **egotistical :** believing that you are much better or more important than other people **angst :** strong feelings of anxiety and unhappiness **on the whole :** in general; in most cases **complicated :** difficult to understand or deal with **counter :** act in opposition to **mass mediation :** exposure to such media

Let's Talk Funny

Ban* Ultra-skinny Models?

Model: We're opposed to the government policy that prevents ultra-skinny models from working in the fashion industry. It's not fair!

Reporter: Why don't you just put on some weight? Then you can work.

Model: No, it's not that easy. Normal women never made the sacrifices we have, but they get all the benefits. We spent years giving ourselves anorexia*, so we can never eat normally again. And the result is that we are permanently unemployed?

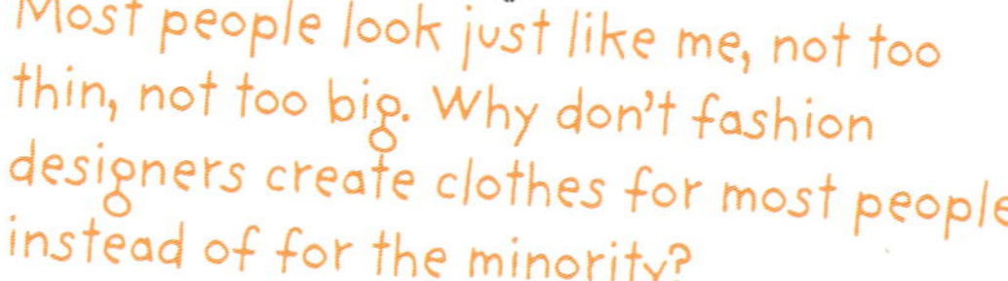

QUESTIONS

1. Should naturally gifted athletes be handicapped in competitions to give ordinary people a chance?
2. Is there something wrong with artificially enhancing one's physical assets in order to compete more successfully (special diets or exercises, weight training, eyeglasses, hearing aids, telescopic sights* or other special equipment like ergonomic* swimsuits, performance enhancing drugs)?
3. If models can be barred* from working because they are too skinny, should basketball players be penalized* because they are too tall? Is there any difference between the two cases?

---

ban : officially or legally prohibit anorexia : lack or loss of appetite for food (as a medical condition) tough : that's too bad — I don't care telescopic sight : optical device that makes distant objects appear larger (It is most often used on rifles to help a shooter aim better at a target.) ergonomics : study of how the design of equipment affects how well, quickly, and comfortably people can use it bar : prevent or forbid (sb) from doing (sth) penalize : give (sb) an unfair disadvantage

Points to Ponder

1

No pressure, no diamond.

2

Stress is the common cold of the psyche*.

3

Under enough pressure, people may admit to murdering a spouse, setting fire to the village church, or robbing a bank, but never to being a bore*.

4

If we could prove the existence of an afterlife*, we would be under less pressure to stay young forever.

---

psyche : (sb's) mind, or their basic nature, which controls their attitude and behavior
bore : uninteresting people
afterlife : (in some religions) life after death

The following sentences are all related thematically. They express a wide difference of opinions and attitudes. You may agree with some of them and disagree with others. Please discuss what you think the sentences mean and what you think about them.

5

There is a phenomenal* amount of pressure on women in this industry: They are considered vintage* by the time they hit their mid-30s.

6

Peer pressure plays a bigger role than romance or security in the desire to get married — or the choice of a spouse.

7

Everybody is under intense pressure to shut up and sing.

8

The pressure of survival in the big city will make you lose sight of your dream. Hang in there*.

---

phenomenal : very great
vintage : old
hang in there : remain determined to succeed, even in a difficult situation

1

The stress is great, but I know I'll come out strong and shining.

2

You fellows worry too much about stress. If you just get on* with things, you never have to worry about it.

get on with : continue doing

3

Give me all your money. Well, no, don't give me your small bills or the big ones, just the ones in the middle. I need too many little bills to buy anything, and so they're heavy to carry around, and the larger bills attract too much attention. So just the middle ones. And hurry up. This gun is heavy. I just got it yesterday and I'm not used to carrying it yet. But people tell me it's very accurate. And deadly. So don't try to do anything clever that will make me suspicious, because I promise I'll shoot. Furthermore,...

I wish he would just shut up and take the money. It's past time for my coffee break.

My arms are tired.

4

I know I'm going to live forever in Heaven, so I might as well relax now as much as I can.

I'm an atheist*, so I need to make every second count* now.

atheist : (sb) who believes that God does not exist
count : be important or valuable

– Pleased to meet you, Mr. Jones. I've heard a lot about you. You're a legend* in this business. And you look so young for your age!
– Thank you. My wife says I should have retired years ago, but I love this work too much to quit. But, I must say, I don't work with many women as old as yourself.
– I'm only 35.
– I don't mean to imply that you look "old," but most women in this industry are right out of college. So, you're exceptional.

legend : famous or important person who is known for doing (sth) extremely well

6

7

in tune : playing or singing the correct musical note

8

I know if I persist, I'll achieve all I want.
I planned my work; I just need to work my plan.

Prejudice

Prejudice means judging in advance, without evidence. In part, it is a mental shortcut* that allows us to make quick decisions without ever having to think about the matter. If Car-Ex Motors makes wonderful automobiles but someone in your family had told you since you were young that they were overpriced, low-quality junkers*, you probably would not ever consider buying one. Unless, of course, one of your friends owned one and you discovered for yourself how wonderful they really are. We also have positive prejudices about things; the point is that we have a pre-formed judgment about a category of things, rather than an empirical*, experience-based knowledge of a particular, individual member of that group. We go through* our lives with these built-in* attitudes, and mostly they are rather harmless. However, we usually use the word "prejudice" to apply to a set of views we hold toward groups of human beings, and usually in a mostly-negative sense. The group may be national, social, cultural, occupational, gender, or any other abstract* set. Anytime we say that "all Martians (or even most Martians) are greedy or kind or good dancers" or give them any other attribute*, we are engaged in prejudice. Because we are not assessing* the qualities of any actual Martian, who may indeed be generous and also cruel but can't dance at all. This kind of prejudice is both unfair and harmful to the person (and group) it is directed toward.

shortcut : quicker way of doing (sth) junker : old car in bad condition empirical : based on testing or experience go through : experience a period or process built-in : forming a natural part of (sb/sth) abstract : based on general ideas or principles attribute : quality or feature assess : make a judgment about (sth) flounder : move in an awkward way with a lot of difficulty and efforts; struggle swamp : land that is always wet and often partly covered with water

Comprehension

1. In your own words, define prejudice. Give an example.
2. How does the article imply* that prejudice can be overcome*?
3. What is wrong with prejudice?

Express Yourself

1. Do we learn prejudice? Or is it inherent* in our nature?
2. If prejudice is a form of ignorance, who do you think is more prejudiced, children or adults? Why do you think so?
3. Are college educated people more prejudiced or less prejudiced than others?
4. Talk about ways of ending the cycle of prejudice.
5. Why is it hard to free ourselves from prejudices?

More Talking Points

What are some common stereotypes about the following?

a. the rich
b. the poor
c. the handicapped
d. the beautiful
e. the ugly
f. fat people
g. men without a college diploma
h. the elderly
i. the young
j. religious people
k. atheists*
l. homosexuals
m. the homeless
n. doctors
o. lawyers
p. politicians
q. the police
r. women with foreign husbands
s. divorcees
t. singles
u. professional athletes
v. ex-convicts*
w. the unemployed

---

imply : express (sth) in an indirect way; suggest (sth) without saying or showing it plainly
overcome : successfully dealt
inherent : belonging to the basic nature of (sb)
atheist : (sb) who believes that God does not exist
ex-convict : former inmate of a prison

Opinion Samples

1. We don't "learn prejudice." We have a natural, inborn tendency to prejudge. The world is too large and complicated for us to ever directly comprehend all of its components, and we have to decide many issues quickly and efficiently. So, we "learn" a specific prejudice. We take at face value* what others tell us, or we use one example from our personal experience and make that the template* for all other members of that class. When we are confronted with counter-examples, we may abandon our earlier prejudice rather quickly, but usually we tend to try to shape the world as it is to the one we imagine it to be as long as we can do so, because it is not easy to change our entire worldview.

2. A diploma does not guarantee wisdom. Some of the dumbest human beings I have ever met are also among the best educated. They have a series of wrongheaded* beliefs about the world and are entirely closed-minded about any other possibilities. Instead of learning in school more about the complexities of life and the need to develop more open-minded, tolerant* attitudes, they use their schooling to find more elaborate* and sophisticated ways of justifying their own prejudice. They become more adept* at using rhetoric* and analogy* to camouflage* their ignorance. They are like the drunkard who uses the lamppost for support rather than enlightenment*.

Dialog

Everybody Thinks What He or She Knows Is Facts, Not Prejudice

Johnny : There must be a thousand reasons I hate my boss.
Phoebe : Really?
Johnny : Yes.
Phoebe : Such as?
Johnny : First off, she's a woman. Women have no place in positions of authority over men. They are too emotional to provide firm leadership.
Phoebe : I resent that! After all, I too am a woman, but I think I run my office rather well.
Johnny : I'm not talking about you. There are always exceptions.
Phoebe : Hmmm. Go ahead.
Johnny : Second, she doesn't have a degree in business or management or economics or, in fact, anything at all to do with the company's business. She's an English major! What does she know about anything real?

---

take (sth) at face value : accept a situation or accept what (sb) says, without thinking there may be a hidden meaning   template : (sth) that serves as a model for others to copy   wrongheaded : having or showing bad judgment; misguided   tolerant : willing to accept feelings, habits, or beliefs that are different from your own   elaborate : made or done with great care or with much detail   adept : very good at doing (sth)   rhetoric : language that is intended to influence people and that may not be honest or reasonable   analogy : comparison of two things based on their being alike in some way   camouflage : hide (sth) by covering it up or making it harder to see   enlightenment : state of having knowledge or understanding

Phoebe : Well, you know, sometimes we select our majors on a whim* or for some transient* reason. Maybe she likes literature. But that doesn't have anything to do with her other interests or abilities. She must have been doing something right or she wouldn't have been promoted, would she?

Johnny : I think she just used her sexuality to her advantage to get herself promoted. I will say one thing good on her behalf: She's a mighty* fine-looking woman!

Phoebe : You're such a sexist*.

Johnny : Don't label me that way. Such prejudice does not become* you.

Phoebe : Okay. Go ahead. What are the other reasons?

Johnny : She comes from a rich family, so she never had to struggle to get ahead. She feels she is entitled to* anything she wants.

Phoebe : Is it her fault if her daddy's got money?

Johnny : Despite her wealth, she couldn't get into a top tier* university. She went to a second-rate school abroad.

Phoebe : Maybe that's because of her interest in English. But certainly living in a foreign culture for a while must be a strong point on anyone's resume.

Johnny : Don't defend her!

Phoebe : Sorry. I didn't mean to. Please continue your senseless rant*.

Johnny : I'm not trying to pick a fight with you.

Phoebe : I know. Go on. What else do you dislike about your boss?

Johnny : She's from the wrong part of the country. The folks there are just not like the rest of us. They're too stubborn* and provincial*.

Phoebe : Living abroad should certainly help counter* any provincialism on her part, and being stubborn might explain her personal success.

Johnny : Please let me finish.

Phoebe : You've got another 995 reasons to go.

Johnny : If you're not going to take me seriously, there's no need for me to keep going.

Phoebe : Okay. I think you've made your point.

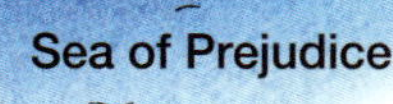

QUESTIONS

1. Do you think Johnny actually has 1,000 reasons, or is that just a figure of speech*?
2. Are any of his points valid*?
3. Should Phoebe be more sympathetic* toward Johnny's feelings?

---

whim : sudden wish, desire, decision, etc. **transient :** not lasting long **mighty :** very
sexist : (sb) who unfairly treats people because of their sex **become :** be appropriate or suitable to (sb)
be entitled to : have the right to have or do (sth) **top tier :** best **rant :** long and angry speech
stubborn : refusing to change your ideas or stop doing (sth) **provincial :** having narrow or limited concerns or interests **counter :** make (sth) less effective or ineffective **figure of speech :** word or expression that is used in a different way from the usual meanings of the words, in order to give you an idea or picture in your mind
valid : fair or reasonable **sympathetic :** showing support for

Read & Discuss

Can We Be Free from Prejudice?

I am a foreigner who has lived abroad most of my adult life and have felt first-hand the effects of prejudice. Because I am a well-educated white American male, the expressions of prejudice have been mostly beneficial*. However, my actual abilities and interests have been largely ignored, and it has been difficult to be accepted for who I am. So, even though the prejudice I have been subjected* to has been generally positive, it has still been corrosive* to my soul. In fairness*, I should also admit to making some wholesale* judgments about the people in my host country. I guess prejudice is a part of human nature, so we cannot ever be entirely free from it. But that does not make it right*.

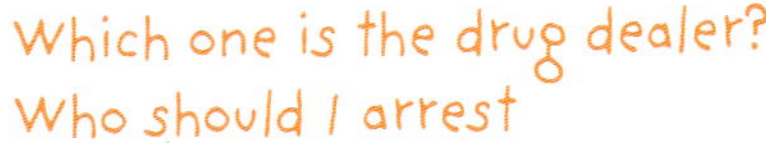

QUESTIONS

1. Have you ever changed your mind about a prejudice you had? Tell us about your experience.
2. Has anyone ever treated you in a certain way, not because of your true nature but because you belong to a certain group? How did that make you feel?
3. Is there anything society can do to reduce prejudice? Is it entirely an individual matter? Is there nothing that can be done?

---

beneficial : producing good or helpful results or effects   subject to : affected by   corrosive : harmful or destructive   in fairness : to be fair   wholesale : broadly indiscriminate   make right : justify   rough : likely to cause harm or injury   cuff : put (sb) in handcuffs

Let's Talk Funny

Social Rejection Could Make You Sick

Man: I have headaches and stomach aches, I can't sleep well, and I am always under a lot of stress.

Doctor: I can take care of those symptoms. Is there anything else, other than these physical conditions?

Man: People don't talk to me. They avoid me and are never interested in me. I don't understand! All I do is put my own interest over theirs. Nobody else is going to look after me if I don't.

Doctor: Okay, I see. Don't worry. I have the perfect prescription. Take these three tablets every morning when you get up and continuously as needed throughout the day, and I guarantee your life will improve: LOVE, UNDERSTANDING, and SELFLESSNESS.

QUESTIONS

1. Would generous dosages of the three tablets solve the man's problem? Why or why not?
2. Is it easy for a selfish person to become an altruist*?
3. If you could concoct* a potion* to enhance* people's understanding, do you think you'd get rich or go broke? Explain your answer.

frame : make (an innocent person) appear to be guilty of a crime **fixed :** predetermined dishonestly **suck :** do (sth) very badly **technicality :** small detail in a rule, law, etc., and esp. one that forces an unwanted or unexpected result **altruist :** (sb) who shows a desire to help other people and a lack of selfishness **concoct :** make (a food or drink) by mixing different things together **potion :** drink intended to have a special or magical effect on the person who drinks it **enhance :** improve

Points to Ponder

1

Since no one can completely read your soul, prejudice will always be part of the way you are evaluated.

2

The bigot* agrees there are two sides to every question—his own and the wrong one.

3

If I thought you were a jerk* before we met, I would be prejudiced. But if we met and I still thought so, I was prophetic*.

4

Prejudice is a great time saver. It enables us to form strong opinions without bothering to get the facts.

---

bigot : (sb) who strongly and unfairly dislikes other people, ideas, etc.
jerk : (sb), esp. a man, who is stupid or who does things that annoy or hurt other people
prophetic : correctly saying what will happen in the future

The following sentences are all related thematically. They express a wide difference of opinions and attitudes. You may agree with some of them and disagree with others. Please discuss what you think the sentences mean and what you think about them.

5

I think people are more susceptible* to prejudice than to reason. Or am I being prejudicial myself by saying so?

6

We should learn to value the differences among us instead of using them to keep score*.

7

Prejudice can't be talked down; it must be lived down.

8

Criticism is prejudice made plausible*.

---

susceptible : easily influenced
keep score : maintain a record of good aspects and bad aspects about (sb), so you can compare them to yourself
plausible : having an appearance of truth or reason; seemingly worthy of approval or acceptance; credible; believable

1

People say I'm conceited* because I have a long nose.
And they say I talk too much, so I have a big mouth.
But I don't think either quality is true in my case.
Only the other big mouths with long noses are like that.

conceited : showing too much pride in your own worth or goodness

2

3

Prejudice has a way of snowballing until it causes an avalanche*.

The path of prejudice and big rocks is determined by gravity, not reason.

avalanche : large amount of snow that slides suddenly down the side of a mountain; sudden great amount of (sth)

4

I was going to get a new watch, but it was too expensive. But this one doesn't require any effort.

But do you think it keeps accurate time? Has it been tested?

Who cares? It looks good and is easy to maintain.

Which one is the prejudiced one?

Is it okay to judge people based on their looks?

I don't know. Is it all right to prejudge on the basis of what somebody says?

Oh! You must be smart, because you don't care anything about your looks.

You must be a clueless* nitwit* or you wouldn't say things like that.

clueless : having no understanding or knowledge of (sth) **nitwit :** stupid or silly person

6

settled : not likely to change
dumb blond : blond women who are not very smart (one of the common prejudices)

7

...low morals. All rich people are selfish, but every poor person is lazy. And foreigners are always ignorant. And...

If I don't hear any ignorant prejudice, maybe it won't exist.

8

I surrender. I'm tired of hearing all these baseless charges.

No wonder they call a dog man's best friend – dogs and men are just alike. They're lazy, they're selfish, and they don't have any conscience. And another thing.....

Me too. It's easier to give up and put up with the prejudice than to waste time and effort to argue against it.

ISSUE 29

Environment

The environment is everything around you that affects your life. You have a family environment — your interactions with your parents, siblings, children, and so forth, and your living conditions — house size, cleanliness, etc. You have a work or school environment, an economic environment, a political environment, and many other environments, that to some extent determine what you can and cannot do. But usually when we speak of an environment we mean our natural physical surroundings — city, jungle, mountains, seaside, agricultural land, whatever — and your climate and weather, and, especially these days, problems associated with pollution and overcrowding. So, an environmentalist is one who monitors these conditions and tries to alleviate* the problems. Some environmentalists are primarily concerned with the extinction* of plant and animal species, some want to preserve natural habitats from economic development, some focus on air and water purity, some are chiefly devoted to noise pollution. Lately, the most intense attention has been placed on the question of "climate change" or "global warming." They refer to* the same phenomenon, but global warming is just one aspect of the larger issue of climate change. As people use more carbon-emitting devices (factories, power plants, and especially petroleum-fuel automobiles) they create a greenhouse effect* within the atmosphere, trapping* solar heat instead of allowing it to escape. As temperatures rise, ice caps* melt and the oceans become larger; and wind patterns and precipitation* rates change as well. So, although the planet as a whole is becoming hotter on average every year, some places may actually become colder.

I'm getting old, I guess. I keep feeling these hot flashes*. I'm not sure if it's because I'm too old or because people on earth are harassing* me. But the problem is that there's no cure for them. I'm on the brink of* exploding.

alleviate : make (sth) less painful, difficult, or severe extinction : disappearance of a whole species refer to : talk about greenhouse effect : warming of the Earth's atmosphere that is caused by air pollution trap : stop (sth) from escaping or being lost ice cap : covering of ice over a large area, esp. on the polar region of a planet precipitation : water that falls to the ground as rain, snow, etc. hot flash : sudden brief hot feeling experienced, esp. by women during menopause harass : annoy or bother (sb) in a constant or repeated way on the brink of : about to experience (sth), typically a disastrous or unwelcome event; very close to

Comprehension

1. How many kinds of environments exist?
2. What do people usually mean when they talk about an environmentalist?
3. What is the difference between global warming and climate change?

Express Yourself

1. What kinds of pollution have you experienced? What have you done about them?
2. Do you think most people are sensitive enough about various pollution issues?
3. Cars and trucks contribute significantly to air pollution. Would you consider buying an electric car in spite of its higher price and greater inconvenience?
4. What do you think about severely limiting automobile use?
5. Nuclear fuel is clean (i.e., non-polluting). Do the safety risks associated with nuclear plants outweigh* their environmental value?
6. Do you think litter* is an important environmental issue? What do you do to prevent it?
7. Separating waste into its various components is one approach to having a cleaner environment. Do you have any reactions to that policy?
8. Even though the government insists that our water supply is safe to drink and free from pollution, many people refuse to drink tap water and buy expensive bottled water instead. Is that reasonable?
9. It takes more than a century for disposable* diapers to decompose*, and meanwhile they are filling our landfills*. Should we discontinue their production?
10. Would you be willing to sacrifice your current standard of living for a cleaner environment? (For example, since cattle add a lot of toxic gas to the air, and also consume more food than they produce, are you willing to cut your meat consumption?)
11. Would you be willing to pay higher taxes for a healthier environment?
12. Do you think our country's anti-pollution laws are tough enough?
13. Are you concerned about other forms of pollution than just bad air and water? What about noise pollution?
14. Do you think urban overcrowding is a form of pollution?
15. Do you think it is okay to leave a sick environment to the next generation to clean up?
16. How can we deal with pollution from neighboring countries if it affects us?
17. Have we crossed the bridge of no return* when it comes to* environmental issues? Can we still save our environment? Or are the environmentalists just alarmists* and exaggerators, and we don't really have much to worry about?

---

outweigh : be greater than (sb/sth) in weight, value, or importance   litter : waste paper, containers etc. that people have thrown away and left on the ground in a public place   disposable : made to be thrown away after one use or several uses   decompose : decay; become rotten   landfill : area where waste is buried under the ground   cross the bridge of no return : make it impossible to return to an earlier state   when it comes to : relating to a particular subject   alarmist : (sb) who spreads unnecessary fear about (sth) that is not truly dangerous

Opinion Samples

1. When we are young, we receive a series of vaccines to inoculate* us against various diseases. The process involves actually receiving the viruses that cause the disease into our bodies, and a tiny number of us actually contract the disease as a result. But we are willing to take that small risk because of the vast benefit that is likely. Similarly, if current consumption levels are indeed unsustainable*, we must be willing to settle for* less or lose everything. I would rather go meatless one day a week than lose my ability to eat steak on any other day. A trivial sacrifice could preserve the much larger privilege I enjoy.

2. The world is a big place. We think it is small because we have seen it from space and we routinely travel from Anywhere to Anywhere Else within a few hours. We have learned much about the interrelatedness* of one part of the planet with all others. So it is easy for us to become alarmed* and think that environmental damage cannot be reversed*. However, as I said, the world is a big place and can accommodate* a great deal of stress. As the atmosphere warms up, the ice sheets melt, and ocean levels rise. So oceans are becoming bigger and their depths will tend to absorb the excess heat. So I'm not worried that we have yet gone too far.

Dialog

NIMBY* Me, NIMBY You

Andre : We need a lot more nuclear facilities if we're ever going to get ahead of the pollution curve*. As long as we depend on coal and oil, we're committing slow-motion suicide.

Elizabeth : You're probably right, in the long run. But where would we put them?

Andre : I don't know. I don't think it's a problem.

Elizabeth : Do you want one in our neighborhood?

Andre : It would probably create jobs here and would be good for the local economy.

Elizabeth : But would it be safe? What about radiation leaks?

Andre : The plants are always being monitored to keep them at safe levels.

Elizabeth : Safe? Even tiny amounts can be fatal or cause birth defects, cancer, sterilization*, and all kinds of health problems. Can it ever be really safe?

---

inoculate : give (sb) a weakened form of a disease in order to prevent infection by the disease
unsustainable : not able to last or continue for a long time settle for (sth) : be happy or satisfied with (sth)
interrelatedness : close relationship alarmed : frightened and worried reverse : cause (sth) to stop or return to an earlier state accommodate : hold comfortably NIMBY : not in my back yard ahead of curve : in a position where you are in control of (sth), and more successful than your competitors sterilization : inability to produce children

Andre : You mean we might get a bunch of mutants* as neighbors?

Elizabeth : Be serious! I wouldn't want my kids to run the constant risk of radiation exposure. Would you?

Andre : No. But they could build a nuclear plant a few miles away and we'd still get the benefits of clean air without having to worry about the risks.

Elizabeth : But somebody else, in a different neighborhood, would still have the same concerns and would probably fight to prevent construction. That's what's known as NIMBY — "not in my back yard."

Andre : I guess that's their problem, after all. But we all have to make sacrifices for the betterment* of society, don't we?

Elizabeth : It's always easier to talk about shared sacrifices when they're all being made by someone else. We get the benefits, but they get the risks. That's an odd kind of sharing!

Andre : Not to change the subject, but I hear you complaining a lot about crime.

Elizabeth : That's right. The laws and the courts are too lenient*. We need to lock up* more offenders and keep them locked up longer!

Andre : So we need more prisons?

Elizabeth : Absolutely!

Andre : Do you want one built next to your house?

Elizabeth : It would certainly negatively affect property values and make the neighborhood less safe.

Andre : So you want more prisons, as long as they're built far away?

QUESTIONS

1. Is there any fair way of deciding where to locate necessary but undesirable facilities?
2. What if a brand new shopping mall were to be constructed where you live, but your home would have to be destroyed for its construction?
3. What if the government were to decide that certain new facilities were necessary and would use a lottery system to determine their placement? Would that be fair and equitable*?

---

mutant : animal or plant that is different in some way from others of the same type, because of a change in its genetic structure that happened by chance **betterment :** improvement **lenient :** not harsh, severe, or strict **lock up (sb) :** imprison (sb) **equitable :** just or fair

Read & Discuss

Priority Provides Privilege. Should It?

The Industrial Revolution began in the United Kingdom and quickly spread throughout western Europe and North America, giving those regions a competitive advantage in terms of living standards, military might*, and economic power. But the rest of the world is finally catching up*. Asia, Africa, and Latin America are no longer "backward" in terms of development. People there are beginning to live longer, healthier lives, with more "luxuries" like automobiles, mobile phones, televisions, computers, and so on. But while the people in these regions are living better lives, they are adding to the overall difficulty of sustaining modern lifestyles across the globe. The older industrialized nations complain that climate change and unregulated pollution from the newly industrializing countries are negatively affecting the living standards of their own citizens, even though their societies have spent decades cleaning up the environment through investment and social control. The new industrialists, however, point out that the older ones had to go through the same dirty, hazardous process in order to reach industrial efficiency; they point out the double standard* of advanced nations: They built industrial systems that benefited themselves at the expense of others but don't want anyone else to live better by adopting the same practices at their expense.

– I insist that you stop!
– What am I doing?
– You're creating pollution. We just spent a fortune trying to clean it up.
– You cleaned up the mess you made yourself, but we had bad air and water as a result, too. Now we're just trying to catch up.
– Do you mean you think it's your turn to act irresponsibly?
– No, but it's our turn to improve our lifestyle.
– Why don't you just stick with* growing rice?
– There's more to life than rice alone. Like giant TVs and unnecessary SUVs.

QUESTIONS

1. If you or your company developed some new process or product, would it be fair to deprive or limit others from deriving* equal benefits from it?
2. If someone developed a cure for cancer, would he be justified in preventing your access to it just because of who you are or where you live (or how much money you have)?
3. If you published a novel and received royalties* on it every year for the rest of your life, maybe that would be fair compensation for your effort. But why should your children and grandchildren continue to benefit after your death? They didn't write it, after all.

Let's Talk Funny

The Nuclear Waste Problem

Reporter: Where can we dispose* of nuclear waste? Nobody wants it nearby.

Politician: Don't worry, I have the solution.

Reporter: Really? What is it?

Politician: You secretly put your waste in someone else's back yard.

Reporter: But what's to prevent others from secretly putting their nuclear waste in your backyard?

Politician: I advocate* that you should have strong protective rights.

QUESTIONS

1. Is the politician's plan fair? Why or why not?
2. What would be wrong (if anything) with launching* nuclear waste into space?
3. Why is nuclear waste more worrisome than other kinds?

---

might : great power or strength, esp. a country's military or economic power **catch up :** reach the same standard as other people **double standard :** rule or principle that is unfairly applied in different ways to different people or groups **stick with :** continue doing (sth) **derive :** get (sth) from (sth) else **royalty :** amount of money that is paid to the original creator of a product, book, or piece of music based on how many copies have been sold

dispose : put (sth) in a particular place **advocate :** support or argue for **YIMBY :** yes in my back yard **launch :** throw

Points to Ponder

1

Only when the last tree has died and the last river poisoned and the last fish been caught will we realize that nature is not infinite.

2

If you really want to appreciate* what an enormous job it is to clean up the environment, start cleaning out your closets.

3

The car industry has finally come up with* a 100-percent-effective anti-pollution device. It's an ignition key that doesn't fit.

4

The sentence "It's too late" is very unsuitable for most environmental issues. It's too late for the dodo* and for people who've starved to death already, but it's not too late to prevent an even bigger crisis. The sooner we act on the environment, the better.

---

appreciate : understand
come up with : think of an idea, plan, etc.
dodo : a clumsy, flightless bird that became extinct

The following sentences are all related thematically. They express a wide difference of opinions and attitudes. You may agree with some of them and disagree with others. Please discuss what you think the sentences mean and what you think about them.

5

Environmental protection doesn't happen in a vacuum*. You can't separate the impact on the environment from the impact on our families and communities.

6

We like to blame the poor for destroying the environment. But the powerful corporations and the government are mostly responsible.

7

Here we are, in a speeding car heading toward a brick wall, and everyone is arguing over where each is going to sit.

8

Politics today is all about false choices: You can have a robust energy economy and a challenged* environment, or a great environment and no economy. That's a false choice. You can do both.

---

in a vacuum : separated from outside events or influences
challenged : impaired or disabled in a specified respect

1

Let me go!
I'm the last fish!

Why should I put you back?
You would just starve to death anyway.

- I started to clean out my closet.
- You didn't get very far.
- I wanted to try on those clothes to see if they still fit.
- If you do that with all your clothes, you'll never get done.
- But it will be fun dressing up all day.

3

– Welcome to the new Eco-Friendly-Mobile. Designed to eliminate all carbon emission.
– But the car won't run!
– That's the only way to do it.

– We destroyed that bug's habitat*. It's doomed*!
– But we can still save the bug. We'll create a new habitat.
– Where?
– We'll tear down* some other habitat.

habitat : place where a plant or animal naturally or normally lives or grows
doomed : completely ruined **tear down** : completely destroy; demolish

5

Greenies : environmentalists **tree hugger :** environmental campaigner (used in reference to the practice of embracing a tree in an attempt to prevent it from being felled)

6

– If you people took more responsibility for your actions, we wouldn't have all these environmental problems.
– It's not our fault. We're just beggars. It's the fault of big business and the government they own.
– It's not our fault! We just give people what they want. But you don't pay any taxes.
– If we had any money to pay taxes on, we'd be grateful.

7

– We finally escaped from all that overcrowding noise and pollution!
– Yes, but I miss my old friends. I'm bored.
– You have me to keep you company. We'll be very happy together.
– But you took the best seat!

8

Social responsibility is a heavy challenge*, but if we work together we can get over* all obstacles*.

Economy
Law
Environment
$
Technology

But it's just the two of us doing all the work. Where is everyone else?

They're waiting for us to load up* their wagons. But they said they'd meet us at the top.

challenge : difficult task **get over :** overcome (a difficulty)
obstacle : (sth) that makes it difficult for you to succeed
load up : put a load of (sth) on or into a vehicle

ISSUE 30

Education

The world of education is changing before our eyes, though we may not yet see what shape it will take. Because of the Internet, very soon a live, in-person teacher will be available only to the poorest students (who cannot afford a computer) and the very richest ones. Everyone in the middle will learn via mouse, keyboard, and terminal. Among the casualties* will undoubtedly be most of the soul-necessary qualities of a traditional liberal education*; understanding the logical descriptiveness of mathematics rather than just its mechanical application; the enrichment to our lives that art, music, and literature bring. Even now, most of us are forced to learn all the wrong things while the important lessons are ignored or neglected. Trigonometry and geometry have never found an application in my life; nor have the quadratic equation or the Pythagorean theorem. Even the memorization of the multiplication tables has been superseded* by the use of any common calculator. The formulae for determining how fast a body falls or for composing sulfur dioxide have long since disappeared from my consciousness (as they should). I never needed to know the difference between a Spenserian and a Shakespearian sonnet. In history classes, we spent far too much time learning the dates of dozens of battles and other events — information that can easily be looked up* on the Internet. Dissecting* frogs and cats has never been an activity I have pursued as an adult, and would probably result in my being arrested if I had. And so it goes*: Most of the knowledge I painfully acquired over more than a decade of my precious youth has proved to be an utter waste of time and effort. What I really needed to learn was why I should be interested at all in learning things (including matters of no practical consequence*), how to develop an active curiosity about the world and how to use the tools at my disposal* (libraries, the worldwide web, etc.) in order to satisfy my curiosity, how to think critically and use my rationality to make basic judgments about the whats and whys of life, how to communicate with others (both as a listener or reader, and as a speaker or writer), and how to live harmoniously with my fellow beings. Instead, in all of these things, I have been left pretty much to my own devices* in trying to figure them out*. And I fear the coming of cyber education will just make matters worse.

I can't rest until I control everything! And then, I'll have to invent something else so I can control it, too!

---

casualty : (sth) that is harmed, lost, or destroyed   liberal education : type of education that encourages you to develop a large range of interests and knowledge and respect for other people's opinions, rather than learning specific technical skills   supersede : take the place of (sb/sth) that is old, no longer useful, etc.
look up : search for   dissect : cut (a plant or dead animal) into separate parts in order to study

Comprehension

1. What useless bits* of knowledge does the author cite?
2. Does the author think those things are of no interest to anybody?
3. What should we all be taught in school?

Express  Yourself

1. Why should we learn?
2. Do you think a college degree is necessary, useful, or unimportant? Explain your answer.
3. A college diploma usually helps its recipient get a better job, but does it help him or her live more happily?
4. Does a diploma ever get in the way* of people having a real life? Discuss your answer.
5. In reality, only a tiny percentage of college graduates get jobs related to their majors. What's wrong with this situation?
6. Some college students drop out of school because they can't afford the expensive tuition. Do you think it's fair? Should the government pay for their entire education? Why or why not?
7. Are teachers important in the educational process? (Yes, but not necessary; of the highest importance; not important at all?)
8. What makes a good teacher so good? What makes a poor teacher poor?
9. What are the parents' roles in education?
10. A little indifference* toward your kids is sometimes said to be the best education for them. Can you explain what that means? Do you agree?
11. Who was/is your chief role model? Why?
12. Did you have a part-time job during your school days? What did you learn from that experience?
13. Would you encourage your children to work while they are in school? Why or why not?
14. Should young children learn a foreign language?
15. How important are the arts (music, drama, painting) and sports in education?
16. Learning is indeed a life-time process. How can we continue to learn after we finish school?

---

and so it goes : and this is how events, life, etc. continued **of no consequence :** without much importance or value **at (sb's) disposal :** available for (sb) to use **leave (sb) to their own devices :** leave (sb) to do as they wish without supervision **figure (sth) out :** understand (sth)

bit : part **get in the way of (sb) :** prevent (sb) from doing (sth) **indifference :** lack of interest or concern

Opinion Samples

1. The best thing that parents can do in educating their kids is to keep out of the way*. Let the qualified, professional teachers train their own students in the prescribed* curriculum. After all, they are the experts, and they are paid to spend all day doing their job, while parents are not specialists and have relatively little time to spend on the subject. Government officials decide overall* educational policy, based on social needs; and the function of school administrators is to implement* that policy and to manage their institutions. It is not the job of parents to get involved in any of these matters. Of course, parents should encourage their kids to do their homework and to study their lessons but beyond that should rarely get involved in the day-to-day learning process.

2. Too often, adults complain that their children are not being taught the basics ("reading, writing, and arithmetic") needed for their future employment prospects, and that schools are wasting a lot of kids' time (and adults' tax money) on frivolous* pursuits. What they fail to realize is that many of these programs, especially in athletics and the arts, are the soul* of an education. They are the subjects that encourage students to explore themselves and their world, they give them an enjoyable break from the drudgery* of rote* learning, and they provide a cultural context for the rest of their lives. They are the parts of school life that students look forward to, even though they might dread* the more formal aspects of classwork.

Dialog

Cutting Back

Harold : Bills! Bills! Bills! Somehow, we need to cut back on our expenses.

Hortense: I agree. For one thing, you should stop going out after work every night, and come home instead.

Harold : I'd like to, but it's a necessary part of work. But I don't see why you need to go out shopping every day. It seems to me you already have everything you need.

Hortense: Once in a while I need to get away from the boredom of household chores or I'll go stir-crazy*. And, mostly, I just go window shopping*. I don't usually buy much.

Harold : I don't suppose we can cut back on utilities, Internet, or cable TV costs.

Hortense: What's the point* of living in the modern world without having modern conveniences?

Harold : I don't want to cut back on our investment program. We'll need that money for our retirement.

Hortense: We should dine out more often.

Harold : How would that save us money?

---

out of the way : in such a position as not to obstruct, hinder, or interfere prescribed : decided by a rule
overall : including or considering everything implement : put into practical effect; carry out
frivolous : not important; not deserving serious attention soul : central or most important part of (sth)
drudgery : boring, difficult, or unpleasant work rote : process of learning (sth) by repeating it many times without thinking about it or fully understanding it dread : fear (sth) that will or might happen
stir-crazy : extremely nervous and upset, esp. because you feel trapped in a place
window shopping : activity of looking at goods in store windows without intending to buy them
point : reason for doing (sth); purpose

Hortense: We wouldn't need to buy as many groceries. And it would reduce the utility bill every month.

Harold : I'll take it under advisement*. But I don't think it would help much.

Hortense: Wait! I have an idea!

Harold : What is it?

Hortense: Let's forget about trying to pay for college diplomas for our kids. That will save us a bundle*!

Harold : That's true. But don't you think it's a necessary expense?

Hortense: They can work their way through school. It would be good for them. They'd learn the value of money and how much work it takes to make it.

Harold : So they would appreciate their diplomas all the more, knowing the sacrifice it entailed.

Hortense: Exactly! It would be for their own good.

Harold : And maybe they won't even have any interest in getting a higher education. There are lots of good jobs that don't need much schooling.

Hortense: Vocational school or junior college might better serve their needs.

Harold : And would certainly be cheaper.

Hortense: And wouldn't take nearly as long. They'd be out in the real world that much sooner, earning their own keep*, raising their own families.

Harold : Taking care of us in our declining years*.

Hortense: A good mechanic makes a lot more than a school teacher or an office worker.

Harold : The military is a good, steady livelihood.

Hortense: Maybe some of them have some singing talent or athletic ability. They could get rich without any schooling at all!

Harold : Or they could get lucky and marry a rich spouse.

Hortense: Or win the lottery!

Harold : I'm glad we had this discussion.

Hortense: Yes, I think for financial reasons we should not pay for our kids' schooling. We'll save a lot of money.

Harold : If we had never had any kids at all, we'd have saved a fortune.

Instead of wasting time in school, I worked out in the gym. I'm going to knock your block off*.

M.A.

You think you're ahead of the game, but before you know it, I'll be your employer.

QUESTIONS

1. A good education does not guarantee a good job. So, why do we invest so much in getting college diplomas?
2. Do you think that, in terms of employment opportunities, having a bachelor's degree is about the same thing as having a high school diploma a generation ago? Discuss your answer.
3. In addition to the diploma itself, what (if anything) do students get in college that is worth the investment?

---

take (sth) under advisement : consider (sth) carefully   bundle : large amount of money
earning your keep : making money you need to pay for food, clothing, a place to live, etc.
(sb's) declining years : last years of (sb's) life   knock (sb's) block off : hit (sb) very hard

Read & Discuss

How to Stay Home from School Without Getting in Trouble

In recent decades, the phenomenon of home schooling has progressed in many societies. Many adults have become increasingly dissatisfied with the quality of public education available, or are unhappy with the social and moral values being inculcated*. So they have decided to take personal responsibility for educating their own children. Of course, the wealthy have often had their offspring educated outside the school system by hiring private tutors, but the difference is that "home schooling" implies that the parents themselves are the teachers. As the demand for this option has grown, so have the standards. Many curricula and materials have been developed that meet the legal educational standards imposed by the larger society, so completing a home schooling course is approximately equivalent* to receiving a high school diploma and is given the same legal status. In addition to having more control over what the child learns, and how well he or she learns it, home schooling parents also have the luxury* of spending far more time and attention on an individual student than any teacher in a crowded classroom can possibly do. And the student can say that his or her teacher truly cares for his or her own progress.

QUESTIONS

1. Do you think students learn better at home or in school?
2. Socialization is an important part of school life. Do home-schooled children have the same opportunity to interact with their peers?
3. Discuss the benefits and disadvantages of teaching your own children at home.

---

inculcate : make (sb) accept an idea by repeating it to them often **equivalent :** equal in value, purpose, rank, etc. **luxury :** (sth) that is helpful or welcome and that is not usually or always available
boss : tell (sb) what to do **torment :** cause to experience severe mental or physical suffering
flunk : give (sb) a failing grade for a test or class

Let's Talk Funny

Corporal Punishment*

Parent: Are you in favor of* corporal punishment?

Teacher: Yes, it is very effective in getting students to behave in a cool, calm, and collected* manner in school.

Parent: But are there any long-term effects?

Teacher: They might become more violent and aggressive later on. But that's someone else's problem, not mine.

QUESTIONS

1. Does corporal punishment just teach children the lesson that violence is the way to resolve* issues?
2. If parents do not inflict* corporal punishment at home, should they allow it to be employed at school?
3. Who (if anyone) should be entrusted* with administering* corporal punishment? A teacher? A school administrator?
4. Even if you think corporal punishment is a good thing, do you think it can be abused*? In what ways?

---

corporal punishment : punishment that involves hitting (sb); physical punishment
in favor of : wanting or approving of (sth) collected : calm and in control of your emotions
resolve : find an answer or solution to (sth) inflict : make (sb) suffer (sth) bad or painful
entrust : give (sb) the responsibility of doing (sth) administer : provide or apply
abuse : use (sth) wrongly

Points to Ponder

1

Raise your words, not your voice. It is rain that grows flowers, not thunder.

2

A man who has never gone to school may steal from a freight car, but if he has a university education, he may steal the whole railroad.

3

It is a thousand times better to have common sense without education than to have education without common sense.

4

I'm not afraid of storms, for I'm learning to sail my ship.

The following sentences are all related thematically. They express a wide difference of opinions and attitudes. You may agree with some of them and disagree with others. Please discuss what you think the sentences mean and what you think about them.

5

It is a miracle that curiosity survives formal education.

6

No man is fully educated until he learns to read himself.

7

Many men are able to solve big problems at the office but are unable to settle little ones at home.

8

An education is expensive, but less so than ignorance.

1

mind : care about or worry about **reasoned :** based on careful thought, and therefore sensible

2

3

With common sense, I can solve most problems confronting* me.

But with an education, I can avoid them altogether.

confronting : facing

4

The wind is picking up*, and the waves are growing larger. I think a storm is brewing*.

I never try to challenge* bad weather. I just find safety inside myself and come out again when it's all over.

pick up : increase in speed or strength brew : start to form
challenge : call to engage in a contest, fight, or competition

5

I know what the book says, but I want to find out for myself.

6

I learned that I can know a lot about someone by listening to his heartbeat.

Before I act, I need to examine my own motives and desires.

7

impunity : freedom from punishment, harm, or loss

8

take some lumps : be badly beaten or hurt **improvise :** do (sth) without any preparation
flexible : willing to change or to try different things

DISCUSSION TEXTBOOKS
FROM LIS KOREA

중고급 어린이 들을 위한 독창적인 영어교재

New Children's Talk (1), (2), (3)

교사용

New Children's Talk (TG)

- 일상생활에서 벌어지는 상황들을 다양한 포맷에 맞추어서 많은 Speaking Chance를 제공합니다.
- 암기 위주의 영어가 아니라 자기 의견을 만들어 낼 수 있는 포맷들을 제공합니다.

청소년의 세계와 그들의 생각 관심사들을 토론으로

Chat Room for Teens (1)(2)(3)

- New Children's Talk를 배운 학생들이 Teen Talk를 쉽게 익힐 수 있는 선행학습교재로 사용할 수 있도록 구성
- 학습의 재미와 능률을 높이기 위해 다양한 그림들과 그것들을 바탕으로 한 토론들 그리고 실제 많은 상황에서 발생하는 대화들과 수많은 지문들을 바탕으로 토론의 다양성을 확보

DISCUSSION TEXTBOOKS
FROM LIS KOREA

자유토론을 위한 훈련과정

Talk Talk Talk (1), (2)

- Express Yourself / Let's Talk / What Do You Think? 과정을 무리 없이 이수하기 위한 예비단계로서 자유토론에 대비하기 위한 많은 훈련과정을 포함하고 있다.
- 여러 상황에 맞는 다양한 질문을 학생들에게 던짐으로써 질문과 응답들의 패턴을 이해하고 습득하게 하고자 했다.
- Express Yourself / Let's Talk / What Do You Think?의 주요 훈련 목표 중 하나인 어떤 영어 단어나 문장을 토론자 스스로 다시 설명하는 훈련에 중점을 두었다.

Talk Talk Talk의 선생님 교재

Teacher's Guide for Talk Talk Talk 1&2

- 기존에 출간 되었던 당사의 교재 Talk Talk Talk 1, 2의 선생님 교재로 출간 되었습니다.
- Talk Talk Talk 1, 2에 나왔던 모든 질문에 대한 정확한 답변과 필요한 경우 찬반 의견들이 모두 제시되어있습니다.

DISCUSSION TEXTBOOKS
FROM LIS KOREA

중고급 토론교재의 결정판

LET'S TALK! (1), (2)

- 실생활과 아주 밀접하고 분명한 의견 대립이 나올 수 있는 주제를 선정 고급 토론 영어를 위한 기초를 가질 수 있도록 구성.
- 토론 영어의 기초 단계인 영어로 설명하는 힘을 길러주기 위해 "What Does It Mean?"을 삽입.
- Question에서는 제시된 주제에 대한 이해력 측정뿐만 아니라 한 주제에 대한 깊이 있는 토론에 대비하는 힘을 길러 주고자 했다.
- Discussion Points에서는 주어진 주제에 대한 토론 포인트는 물론이고 그와 연관된 많은 주제 제공
- Opinion Samples에서는 학습자들이 주어진 주제에 대해 토론을 준비할 수 있도록 만은 찬반 의견과 참고 의견들을 제시하고 있다.
- 어려운 표현이나 Idiomatic Expressions에 대해 각주에 충분한 영어 설명을 달아 학습자들로 하여금 이해가 쉽도록 하였다.

설명간결한 형식의 새로운 토론교재

Express Yourself Directly (1), (2)

- Pictures Talk 섹션에서는 큰 주제에 대한 warm-up 주제들을 선정하여 그림과 함께 제시하여 본 주제에 쉽게 접근할 수 있도록 했습니다.
- Express Yourself Directly 섹션에서는 Pictures Talk 섹션에서 다루지 않은 좀 더 깊은 주제를 선정하여 심도 있는 토론이 되도록 했습니다.
- Let's Talk Funny 색션에서는 본 주제와 관련있는 재미 있는 이야기를 실어 가벼운 토론과 함께 긴장을 풀도록 했습니다.
- What Does It Mean?에서는 본 주제와 관련된 Food For Thought를 제공하여 학습자들이 자유롭게 토론 할 수 있도록 했으면 다양한 의견이 나올 수 있는 문구들을 제시하였습니다.
- 마지막으로 Synopsis에서는 (전체 400의 그림으로 구성) 각 그림에 대한 설명을 영어로 명쾌하게 제시하여 학습자가 주제에 대한 최종 복습을 할 수 있도록 했습니다.

EXPRESS YOURSELF 2

– 3rd Edition –

3판 1쇄 인쇄 : 2018년 6월 20일 인쇄
3판 1쇄 발행 : 2018년 6월 25일 발행
지 은 이 : 리스 코리아 편집부 & Duane Vorhees
펴 낸 곳 : (도서출판) 리스코리아
펴 낸 이 : 조은예
등 록 : 남양주 제 399-2011-000003호
전 화 : (0502) 423-7947
편 집 디 자 인 : 이명금, 전정애
일러스트레이터 : 김나나
인 쇄 : (주)미광원색

www.liskorea.com

Shopping doesn't have to be hard work. I can get anything I want online, find the best price, take a break while I surf the net, watch a sports event, and chat with my friends. And I can do it all in the quiet of my own home, especially if my wife is out with her friends.

Who's the real dummy?

I'll never understand my husband. He just wants to stay home and play with his computer. But he's missing out on a lot of excitement—looking at all the new store items, imagining what I'd look like in a nice gown I see, talking with my friends, relaxing over coffee, getting some exercise. It's a whole afternoon of excitement, and usually I don't spend anything.

Look at that dress! Don't you think it suits me? And it's on sale, too! Let's take a look.

At my age, this is getting to be hard work. I should have gone into my father's old trade, pickpocketing. The hours are better, and there's no mandatory* retirement age.
I didn't believe it when they told me hacking was like printing money. The hours are flexible, I can do it at my leisure*, and I don't even have to leave home.

– I insist that you stop!
– What am I doing?
– You're creating pollution. We just spent a fortune trying to clean it up.
– You cleaned up the mess you made yourself, but we had bad air and water as a result, too. Now we're just trying to catch up.
– Do you mean you think it's your turn to act irresponsibly?
– No, but it's our turn to improve our lifestyle.
– Why don't you just stick with* growing rice?
– There's more to life than rice alone. Like giant TVs and unnecessary SUVs.

You won't believe what I'm seeing! There's somebody driving a horse and buggy down the main street.
Why is that man talking to himself? Is he crazy?
Excuse me, young man. We seem to have made a wrong turn. Can you direct us back to our home?
Do I look like some kind of human map? And who's going to clean up that horse's mess?